Communications
in Computer and Information Science 2019

Rationale

The CCIS series is devoted to the publication of proceedings of computer science conferences. Its aim is to efficiently disseminate original research results in informatics in printed and electronic form. While the focus is on publication of peer-reviewed full papers presenting mature work, inclusion of reviewed short papers reporting on work in progress is welcome, too. Besides globally relevant meetings with internationally representative program committees guaranteeing a strict peer-reviewing and paper selection process, conferences run by societies or of high regional or national relevance are also considered for publication.

Topics

The topical scope of CCIS spans the entire spectrum of informatics ranging from foundational topics in the theory of computing to information and communications science and technology and a broad variety of interdisciplinary application fields.

Information for Volume Editors and Authors

Publication in CCIS is free of charge. No royalties are paid, however, we offer registered conference participants temporary free access to the online version of the conference proceedings on SpringerLink (http://link.springer.com) by means of an http referrer from the conference website and/or a number of complimentary printed copies, as specified in the official acceptance email of the event.

CCIS proceedings can be published in time for distribution at conferences or as post-proceedings, and delivered in the form of printed books and/or electronically as USBs and/or e-content licenses for accessing proceedings at SpringerLink. Furthermore, CCIS proceedings are included in the CCIS electronic book series hosted in the SpringerLink digital library at http://link.springer.com/bookseries/7899. Conferences publishing in CCIS are allowed to use Online Conference Service (OCS) for managing the whole proceedings lifecycle (from submission and reviewing to preparing for publication) free of charge.

Publication process

The language of publication is exclusively English. Authors publishing in CCIS have to sign the Springer CCIS copyright transfer form, however, they are free to use their material published in CCIS for substantially changed, more elaborate subsequent publications elsewhere. For the preparation of the camera-ready papers/files, authors have to strictly adhere to the Springer CCIS Authors' Instructions and are strongly encouraged to use the CCIS LaTeX style files or templates.

Abstracting/Indexing

CCIS is abstracted/indexed in DBLP, Google Scholar, EI-Compendex, Mathematical Reviews, SCImago, Scopus. CCIS volumes are also submitted for the inclusion in ISI Proceedings.

How to start

To start the evaluation of your proposal for inclusion in the CCIS series, please send an e-mail to ccis@springer.com.

Jun Qi · Po Yang

Editors

Internet of Things of Big Data for Healthcare

5th International Workshop, IoTBDH 2023
Birmingham, UK, October 21–25, 2023
Proceedings

 Springer

Editors
Jun Qi 🆔
Xi'an Jiaotong-Liverpool University
Suzhou, China

Po Yang 🆔
University of Sheffield
Sheffield, UK

ISSN 1865-0929   ISSN 1865-0937 (electronic)
Communications in Computer and Information Science
ISBN 978-3-031-52215-4   ISBN 978-3-031-52216-1 (eBook)
https://doi.org/10.1007/978-3-031-52216-1

This Springer imprint is published by the registered company Springer Nature Switzerland AG
The registered company address is: Gewerbestrasse 11, 6330 Cham, Switzerland

Paper in this product is recyclable.

Preface

This volume contains papers from the 5th International Workshop on Internet of Things of Big Data for Healthcare (IoTBDH 2023), which was held under the 2023 International Conference on Information and Knowledge Management (CIKM). The workshop was held on 22nd October 2023 in Birmingham, UK.

Internet of Things (IoT) enabled technology has rapidly and efficiently facilitated healthcare diagnosis and treatment with low-cost and lightweight devices. Big data generated from IoT offers valuable and crucial information to guide decision-making, improve patient outcomes, decrease healthcare costs, etc. The workshop aimed to provide an opportunity for researchers and practitioners from both academia and industry to present state-of-the-art research and applications in utilizing IoT and big data technology for healthcare by presenting efficient scientific and engineering solutions, addressing the needs and challenges of integration with new technologies, and providing visions for future research and development. The 1st IoTBDH was held in 2015 as a workshop under the 2015 IEEE International Conference on Computer and Information Technology; Ubiquitous Computing and Communications; Dependable, Autonomic and Secure Computing; Pervasive Intelligence and Computing (CIT/IUCC/DASC/PICOM). The 2nd IoTBDH was held in 2017 under the 2017 IEEE International Conference on Internet of Things (iThings), IEEE Green Computing and Communications (Green-Com), IEEE Cyber, Physical and Social Computing (CPSCom), and IEEE Smart Data (SmartData). The 3rd IoTBDH, held in 2018, was under the IEEE 20th International Conference on High Performance Computing and Communications; IEEE 16th International Conference on Smart City; IEEE 4th International Conference on Data Science and Systems (HPCC/SmartCity/DSS). The 4th IoTBDH was held in 2020 under the 2020 IEEE Intl. Conf. on Parallel & Distributed Processing with Applications; Big Data & Cloud Computing; Sustainable Computing & Communications; Social Computing & Networking (ISPA/BDCloud/SustainCom/SocialCom). This year, we were pleased that the 5th IoTBDH was held in Birmingham, UK.

We received a total of 36 submissions, six times the number at the previous workshop. Each submission was peer reviewed by two reviewers from our Program Committee (PC) as well as sub-reviewers invited by our PC members, resulting in 70 reviews. All reviews were double-blind, and submissions not properly anonymized were desk-rejected without review. Based on the review scores and confidence levels of the reviewers, 7 submissions were accepted as full papers and 4 as short papers. These 11 manuscripts were authored by 116 scholars and graduates students.

IoTBDH 2023 would not have been possible without the contributions and efforts of a dedicated scientific community. We sincerely appreciate members of our Program Committee and all the external reviewers for providing comprehensive and timely reviews. We also appreciate the funding support of the Young Scientists Fund of the National Natural Science Foundation of China (62301452), the China Scholarship Council (202107030007), and the Engineering and Physical Sciences Research Council

(EPSRC) Doctoral Training Partnership (EP/T517835/1). The conference management system EasyChair was used to handle the submissions and conduct the reviewing and deciding. We thank Springer for their continued trust and for publishing the proceedings of IoTBDH 2023.

December 2023   Jun Qi
                                                    Po Yang

Organization

Workshop Organizers

Jun Qi	Xi'an Jiaotong-Liverpool University, China
Po Yang	University of Sheffield, UK

Programme Committee

Jun Qi	Xi'an Jiaotong-Liverpool University, China
Po Yang	University of Sheffield, UK
Hongqing Yu	University of Derby, UK
Yun Yang	Yunnan University, China
Zhibo Pang	KTH Royal Institute of Technology, Sweden

Additional Reviewers

Tong Liu	Kang Liu
Fengtao Nan	Yu Zhang
Jianjun Chen	Menghui Zhou
Xulong Wang	Haoyu Wu

Contents

Enhancing Search Engine Optimization in Healthcare and Clinical
Domains with Natural Language Processing and Graph Techniques 1
    Soodabeh Sarafrazi, Darwin Wheeler, David Garcia, Shane Henrikson,
    Naveed Sharif, and Hui Wu

Evaluation of Integrated XAI Frameworks for Explaining Disease
Prediction Models in Healthcare 14
    Hong Qing Yu, Adebola Alaba, and Ebere Eziefuna

Zero-Shot Medical Information Retrieval via Knowledge Graph
Embedding 29
    Yuqi Wang, Zeqiang Wang, Wei Wang, Qi Chen, Kaizhu Huang,
    Anh Nguyen, and Suparna De

Deep Recognition of Chinese Herbal Medicines Based on a Caputo
Fractional Order Convolutional Neural Network 41
    Tao Li, Jiawei Yang, Chenxi Li, Lulu Lv, Kang Liu, Zhipeng Yuan,
    Youyong Li, and Hongqing Yu

Randomized Multi-task Feature Learning Approach for Modelling
and Predicting Alzheimer's Disease Progression 52
    Xulong Wang, Yu Zhang, Menghui Zhou, Tong Liu, Zhipeng Yuan,
    Xiyang Peng, Kang Liu, Jun Qi, and Po Yang

Adaptive Prior Correction in Alzheimer's Disease Spatio-Temporal
Modeling via Multi-task Learning 69
    Xiangchao Chang, Menghui Zhou, Yun Yang, and Po Yang

An Electromyographic Signal Acquisition System for Sarcopenia 84
    Yihui Jian, Kaitai Mao, Jing Chen, Xinrui Ling, Ziguan Jin, Zhiqiu Ye,
    Geng Yang, Qin Zhang, and Kaichen Xu

Machine Learning-Based Metabolic Syndrome Identification 94
    Chang Liu, Jingjing Liu, Zhangdaihong Liu, and Yang Yang

A Comparative Study of ResNet and DenseNet in the Diagnosis of Colitis
Severity 102
    Chenxi Li, Jiawei Yang, Yuxin Qin, Lulu Lv, and Tao Li

Removal of EOG Artifact in Electroencephalography with EEMD-ICA:
A Semi-simulation Study on Identification of Artifactual Components 111
  Jingzhou Xu, Wengyao Jiang, Wei Wang, Jianjun Chen, Yixiao Shen,
  and Jun Qi

Representative UPDRS Features of Single Wearable Sensor for Severity
Classification of Parkinson's Disease 124
  Yuting Zhao, Xulong Wang, Xiyang Peng, Ziheng Li, Fengtao Nan,
  Menghui Zhou, Peng Yue, Zhong Zhao, Yun Yang, and Po Yang

Author Index 137

Enhancing Search Engine Optimization in Healthcare and Clinical Domains with Natural Language Processing and Graph Techniques

Soodabeh Sarafrazi[1], Darwin Wheeler[2], David Garcia[2], Shane Henrikson[2], Naveed Sharif[2], and Hui Wu[2(✉)]

[1] Oakland 94612, USA
[2] Kaiser Permanente, Oakland 94612, USA
{darwin.s.wheeler,david.x3.garcia,shane.a.henrikson,
naveed.sharif,jason.x2.wu}@kp.org

Abstract. Search Engine Optimization (SEO) is the art of refining a website to enhance its visibility in search engine results, capturing the attention of both potential and existing customers. At Kaiser Permanente Digital, our unwavering commitment is to provide individuals with pertinent and precise health-related information. In this study, our primary objective is to elevate the rankings of KP.org webpages. To attain this goal, we leverage data from a third-party platform and harness cutting-edge Natural Language Processing (NLP) techniques, including the powerful large language model BERT. Our NLP arsenal encompasses diverse techniques, such as clustering and topic modeling, designed to extract invaluable insights from our data. Moreover, we complement our findings with practical examples and compelling visualizations tailored to the clinical and healthcare domain. Additionally, we conduct thorough graph analysis, employing methods like node2vec, to identify pages with closely related content within our domain, addressing the issue of keyword cannibalization and content competition for ranking. In this paper, we present our innovative solutions in a visually intuitive manner, showcasing how these approaches not only optimize our content effectively but also ensure strategic and non-redundant keyword utilization across our website.

Keywords: Search Engine Optimization (SEO) · Natural Language Processing (NLP) · Large Language Model (LLM) · Graph Analysis

1 Introduction

At Kaiser Permanente (KP) Digital, our ongoing effort is to deliver relevant and accurate health-related information to people. In this study, our goal is to enhance the rankings of KP.org domain pages. By leveraging diverse machine learning techniques, our goal is to

S. Sarafrazi—Independent Researcher.

J. Qi and P. Yang (Eds.): IoTBDH 2023, CCIS 2019, pp. 1–13, 2024.
https://doi.org/10.1007/978-3-031-52216-1_1

empower SEO and content generation teams in creating enhanced content and webpage structures. This, in turn, will boost the visibility and accessibility of our health-related content.

The first problem with KP.org domain pages is the lack of sufficient content. This insufficiency can negatively impact SEO by impeding search engines' ability to assess the pages' relevance and quality for specific search queries. Consequently, it can result in lower search rankings for those pages. To address this problem, it is essential to enhance the content by offering comprehensive and informative knowledge that fulfills user intent. This optimization will increase the likelihood of achieving higher rankings in search engine results, thereby attracting more clicks from users. It is widely observed that people tend to click on search results that appear at the top positions in the rankings.

The second problem with KP.org domain pages is the presence of pages with highly similar content, resulting in keyword cannibalization. Such phenomenon occurs when multiple pages within a website target the same keyword or set of keywords. This confusion confounds search engines and has a detrimental effect on SEO efforts. To mitigate this issue, it is important to review and optimize the content of each page, ensuring that each targets unique keywords and offers distinct, valuable information. By doing so, search engines can better understand the relevance of each page, leading to improved SEO performance. In this study, we are leveraging state of the art machine learning techniques to address the issue of insufficient content on KP.org domain pages and effectively tackle keyword cannibalization.

2 Literature Review

The evolution of artificial intelligence (AI) has empowered search engine developers to continuously enhance their algorithms. They employ a variety of these methods to acquire accurate data and fulfill user expectations. These methods encompass Self-Organizing Map [1], Forest Generation Algorithm [2], and Support Vector Machine [3]. Additionally, search engines take numerous factors into account when determining website rankings on the internet. For instance, Google relies on more than 200 undisclosed factors [1], and even if these factors were fully disclosed, the specific weighting and algorithms used to evaluate each one remains undisclosed. More recently, Google has confirmed the implementation of RankBrain, an artificial intelligence component that plays a pivotal role in shaping search engine rankings [4, 5].

Utilizing AI techniques to procure precise data from search engines poses an enduring challenge for SEO professionals, requiring a profound grasp of search engine algorithms for effective adaptation. This is where AI, ML, and NLP methods prove invaluable. Here, we will provide a summary of various endeavors that amalgamate these technologies with SEO. The existing literature at the intersection of machine learning and SEO is somewhat limited. Nevertheless, we have uncovered several studies that delve into this domain.

In a literature review conducted by Yuniarthe [6], a comprehensive exploration of AI applications in SEO was undertaken. This review uncovered various prototypes such as Polidoxa and Fuzzy Inference System, along with the adoption of commercial packages like SPSS Clementine and SearchDex Hyperloop. Additionally, the application of Support Vector Machine and the K-Nearest Neighbor Algorithm were discussed. However, it was noted that challenges in this research domain arise from the inherent confidentiality of SEO company algorithms and the constraints imposed by search engines.

Godlevsky et al. [7] proposed a theoretical basis for SEO utilizing situation control, machine learning, semantic net building, data mining, and service-oriented architecture. The approach was validated through successful SEO projects in Ukraine from 2012 to 2016. Salminen et al. [8] utilized 30 ranking factors and an XGBoost model to predict page rankings for 733 content pages, achieving an accuracy of 0.86. Links and website security were found to be important ranking factors. Drivas et al. [9] introduced a predictive model that integrates statistical findings and utilizes both a macro-level descriptive model and a micro-level data-driven agent-based model. The aim was to devise effective strategies that enhance the visibility and discoverability of cultural collections on the Internet. Portier et al. (2020) [10] analyzed the performance of different machine learning models applied to selected features for search engine ranking. The Random Forest model combined with the Fisher filter method or Backward Elimination wrapper method yielded the best results.

In light of the development of large language models and the continuous advancements in NLP, it's evident that natural language understanding plays a paramount role, if not the most crucial, in machine learning algorithms utilized by search engines. Consequently, we present a collection of studies dedicated to exploring the practical applications of NLP in the context of content optimization within the domain of SEO.

In their comprehensive study, Vinutha [11] examined the synergy between Machine Learning (ML) and NLP in SEO. This study shows that NLP enhances natural language understanding but faces challenges with quantitative factors like keyword density and backlinks. ML excels in data analysis and ranking predictions. The author proposes a combined approach, utilizing NLP for query understanding and ML for ranking predictions, as a potent strategy for effective SEO.

In a study conducted by Reutterer et al. [12], the authors delved into the application of natural language generation (NLG) within the context of content marketing for SEO. Their investigation centered on the utilization of NLG to autonomously generate website landing page content. Through field experiments conducted across two distinct industries, their findings unveiled the potential of machine-generated SEO content to surpass human-authored content in terms of search engine rankings. Moreover, this approach demonstrated a remarkable reduction in production costs, thereby substantially enhancing Return on Investment (ROI) in the domain of content marketing.

In their study, Jenkins et al. [13] devised a model to generate text annotations tailored for SEO. This model leverages the Extreme Gradient Boosting algorithm to accurately label phrases and utilizes logistic regression to generalize rankings for content clusters. Their research results highlight that the proposed model leads to a noticeable increase in web content traffic, typically in the range of 1–2%.

Sharma et al. [14] introduce an innovative semantic architecture that harnesses web and data mining techniques to enhance eCommerce search engine personalization. The architecture's development involves several key phases. Firstly, it conducts query expansion using NLP operations to grasp the user's intent. Following that, an ontology classification step filters relevant web content subjects. Subsequently, topic modeling through clustering is employed, and statistical computations are utilized for effective re-ranking.

Horasan [15] implements latent semantic analysis for SEO purposes. This study involves extracting keywords from textual data through latent semantic analysis, a technique that establishes connections between documents, sentences, and terms within the text using principles of linear algebra.

In our paper, we leverage the widely recognized Bidirectional Encoder Representations from Transformers (BERT) model [16], which is extensively employed by Google, the predominant search engine globally. Our focus revolves around the intricate challenge of optimizing content within the SEO context. To the best of our knowledge, this research marks a unique endeavor, being among the first to explore the application of the BERT model in deciphering user query intents for content enhancement in the SEO domain.

Moreover, we take a pragmatic step forward by tackling the complex issue of keyword cannibalization. Through the utilization of graph analysis, we offer a practical solution. In essence, our study endeavors to address two primary concerns faced by SEO professionals. Our approach is grounded in real-world applicability, providing insights and resolutions that can assist practitioners in their day-to-day work. This distinctive combination of BERT-based content optimization and graph-based keyword cannibalization management in the clinical and healthcare domain sets our research apart within the SEO landscape.

3 Data

In this study, we draw upon a comprehensive third-party keyword research dataset, encompassing several vital components. This dataset comprises the keyword itself, search volume (reflecting the frequency of searches for each keyword), difficulty (gauging the level of competition for securing a place on search engine result pages), URLs of pages within the KP.org domain, alongside their corresponding rankings. Additionally, it includes URLs and rankings for competitor pages. This rich dataset serves as a crucial resource, affording us valuable insights into the keywords' popularity and competitiveness, enabling the evaluation of the performance of KP.org domain pages, and facilitating an in-depth analysis of competitor pages' rankings and strategies.

Within the dataset employed for this research, we encountered a robust collection of 115,000 queries related to cancer in a broader context. These queries represent the actual searches conducted by users within a single month, specifically, August 2022, through major search engines such as Google and Bing.

4 Methods

In this study, our focus is on addressing two critical problems: content optimization and keyword cannibalization, as mentioned earlier. To tackle the first problem, we utilize techniques such as word frequency analysis, word combination exploration, query clustering and topic modeling. For the second challenge concerning keyword cannibalization, we employ graph analytics methodologies.

4.1 Keyword Frequency and Network Analysis

To address the first problem (content optimization), we use the bag-of-words method to identify the most frequent words associated with each topic. We then take it one step further and employ network analysis to uncover the most frequent combinations of words.

4.2 Hierarchical Clustering and Topic Modeling

We also employ clustering techniques to identify similar queries based on their intent using BERT [16]. Google search engine utilizes BERT, a cutting-edge Large Language Model (LLM), to understand and fulfill user search queries [5]. BERT is employed to generate vector representations of keywords, which are then clustered together using a hierarchical clustering algorithm. This clustering process helps identify queries with similar intents. By grouping related terms, we can identify high-potential clusters that can attract website traffic based on their total search volume and average keyword difficulties. These two methods work in tandem to enhance our content optimization efforts. To perform topic modeling, we utilize the BERTopic library [17]. BERTopic is a powerful approach that leverages transformers and c-TF-IDF to generate dense clusters. This methodology facilitates the creation of easily interpretable topics while ensuring that important words are retained within the topic descriptions.

4.3 Page Clustering Using Graph Techniques

To address the challenge of internal content cannibalization within the KP.org domain, we harness the prowess of graph techniques. In this intricate analysis, each webpage within the KP.org domain and those of our competitors (e.g., competitor 1, competitor 2) are depicted as nodes within a comprehensive graph. A link is forged between two nodes when both pages share ranking for a specific keyword, with the strength of this link determined by the extent of their shared keywords. This method births an undirected graph replete with weighted edges.

To pinpoint nodes exhibiting remarkable similarity within this intricate network, we employ the node2vec algorithm [18]. Node2vec deftly distills low-dimensional vector representations of nodes by assimilating the intricacies of the graph's structural tapestry. In doing so, it unveils the parallels between nodes through their interconnections and the commonality of keywords they embrace. Through this innovative fusion of NLP, ML, and graph techniques, we embark on a journey to decipher and conquer the intricate labyrinth of content optimization and keyword strategy in the ever-evolving landscape of SEO.

5 Results

5.1 Keyword Frequency and Network Analysis

Figures 1, 2, 3, 4, 5 and 6 are screenshots of the interactive Microsoft PowerBI dashboard [19] that we have developed. The bag-of-words method result for breast cancer topic is visualized in Fig. 1. Here we see the 30 most frequent words that users search for in relation to breast cancer.

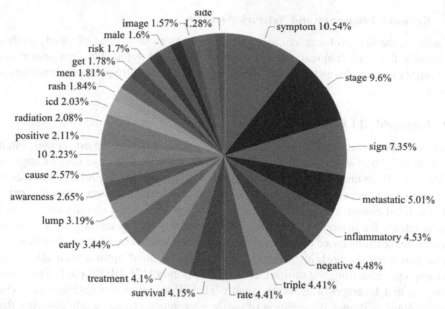

Fig. 1. Most Frequent Keywords Related to Breast Cancer

Figure 2, illustrates the network analysis results, showcasing the interconnectedness and prevalence of specific word combinations within the data. Using this analysis, we can identify the frequent words and determine the accompanying most common words associated with each of them. This analysis provides writers and content generators with a valuable insight into the interconnectedness of important words within the context of breast cancer. Such understanding enables them to develop a more comprehensive grasp of the relationships between key terms and enhance their content accordingly.

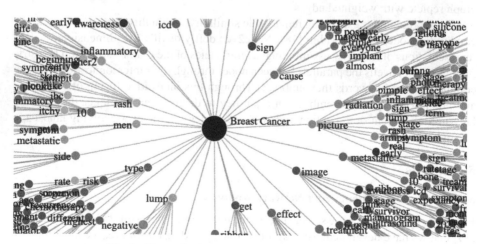

Fig. 2. Network of Keywords Related to Breast Cancer

In Fig. 3, we present a closer view of one of the frequently occurring words displayed in the interactive visualization of Fig. 2: "lump." This illustration showcases the associated terms related to this word. The visual aims to address the queries that content generators may have regarding users' interests in relation to this keyword. By examining the visual, we can observe the users' curiosity about various aspects of a lump, such as its presence in the armpit, potential pain, or discomfort, and whether it is cancerous. The varying size of the circles within the network is directly linked to the search volume associated with each term. This visualization not only offers content generators the most critical and frequently used keywords but also provides valuable insights into important topics they can explore for each of them. This comprehensive approach enables them to address user interests effectively and generate meaningful and engaging material related to the identified keywords.

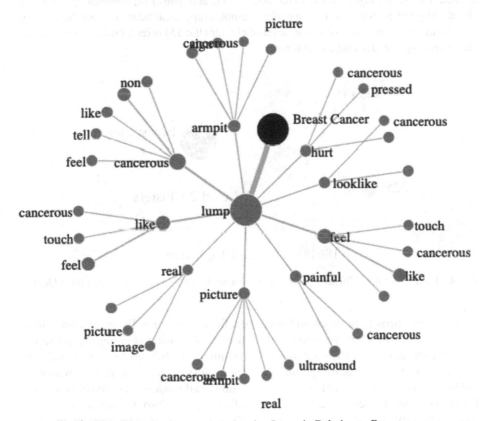

Fig. 3. Most Frequent Keywords Related to Lump in Relation to Breast cancer

5.2 Hierarchical Clustering

As described in Sect. 4, our approach involves utilizing BERT embeddings and hierarchical clustering to group queries into highly similar intent clusters. By adjusting the clustering threshold, we can control the proximity of intent within each cluster. While smaller clusters with closely related queries serve specific purposes, such as identifying "Golden Opportunities" (which will be discussed later), content generators often require a broader perspective. To accommodate this need, we generate different levels of clusters by employing various threshold levels, allowing for a more comprehensive understanding of query intent across different scales.

Figure 4, provides an illustrative example of a hierarchical cluster structure. The cluster with ID = 15 (Level 2) comprises three smaller clusters, namely ID = 1233, ID = 325, and ID = 1861 (Level 1), which consist of queries sharing very similar intents. For a more comprehensive understanding of this arrangement, please refer to Table 1. This table presents a selection of query examples from the hierarchy of clusters depicted in Fig. 4. It demonstrates the diverse levels of clusters that cater to different scales of intents. The initial layer clusters (ID: 352, 1233, and 1861) predominantly focus on closely aligned intents, such as specific chemotherapy treatments or specific type of breast cancer. In contrast, the higher level of cluster (ID: 15) offer a broader perspective, encompassing a wider range of intents.

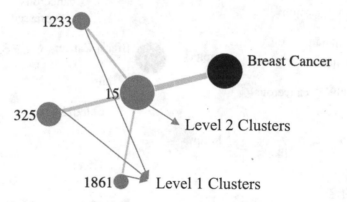

Fig. 4. The Hierarchy of Clusters Exhibits Different Scales of Similarities Among Inner Queries

Figure 5, sheds light on an additional benefit of clustering. By organizing related keywords with similar intents into Level 1 Clusters (as illustrated in Fig. 4), and subsequently evaluating them based on their search volume and difficulty, we unveil valuable prospects known as "golden opportunities." These clusters, depicted in Fig. 5 within the red box, exhibit a considerable total search volume and moderate keyword difficulties. Recognizing these intents enables us to identify topics that have the potential to attract significant traffic to our websites. In the specific context of breast cancer, our analysis has identified over 40 clusters that belong to this category.

In this analysis, it is crucial to understand that, for BERT to correctly comprehend the intent of a query, we should refrain from employing techniques like stemming, lemmatization, or the exclusion of stop words, as is common in many other NLP tasks. Therefore, in our initial approach, we input these queries to the BERT model without any alterations.

Table 1. Example of Queries in Different Cluster Levels

Query	Cluster Level 1 ID	Cluster Level 2 ID
carboplatin and taxol breast cancer	325	15
carboplatin and taxotere for breast cancer	325	15
carboplatin breast cancer	325	15
carboplatin chemotherapy breast cancer	325	15
xeloda breast cancer	1233	15
xeloda breast cancer adjuvant	1233	15
xeloda and metastatic breast cancer	1233	15
xeloda triple negative breast cancer	1861	15
xeloda for residual triple-negative breast cancer	1861	15
xeloda triple negative breast cancer	1861	15

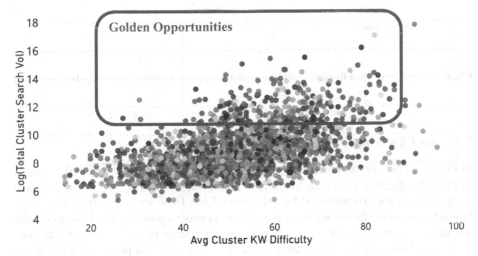

Fig. 5. Cluster Analysis - Search Volume vs Keyword Difficulty

Through this method, we achieved a remarkable performance of 95% for our intent clusters (level 1), as evaluated by humans. This implies that in 95% of the clusters, all queries within a cluster address the same intent. In the remaining 5%, we encountered two types of issues. First, not all queries within one cluster referred to a single intent. Second, in very few cases, two clusters addressed the same intent. Upon analyzing these clusters, we identified misspelling as the root cause of these issues.

To enhance the accuracy of our clustering in the second round, we addressed these spelling issues with the assistance of Python libraries, particularly a library called pyspellchecker [20]. Following this round of spell correction, we achieved an impressive accuracy rate of 99%.

5.3 Topic Modeling

Through a distinct analysis, we utilize BERT topic modeling to ascertain the topic with the most significant search volumes. Figure 6 depicts a two-dimensional visualization showcasing the top 20 topics. The size of the circles in the visualization corresponds to their respective search volumes, providing a visual representation of their significance.

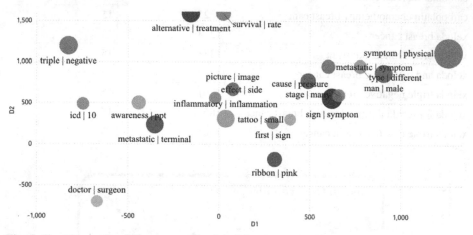

Fig. 6. Two-Dimensional Representation of the Most Important Topics Related to Breast Cancer

5.4 Page Clustering

In Fig. 7, we observe an embedding of nodes representing three entities: KP.org pages (represented by blue nodes), competitor 1 pages (represented by yellow nodes), and competitor 2 pages (represented by red nodes). Let's focus on a specific KP.org page labeled as K8 in the figure. K8 is the main breast cancer page within the KP.org domain, intended to comprehensively address a wide range of queries related to this topic. Despite its intended purpose, the effectiveness of K8 is hindered by the presence of numerous competing minor pages and even PDF files within the domain. As a result, the desired level of traffic cannot be achieved through this page.

Using page clustering we can detect nodes (pages) very similar to K8. These nodes fall into two categories. Firstly, we have nodes within the KP.org domain, which represent pages that are highly similar to K8. These pages contribute to keyword cannibalization, as they compete for the same keywords and can potentially dilute the visibility and ranking of K8. Secondly, we have nodes in competitors' domains. These nodes offer valuable insights into how our competitors address a specific topic. By examining the pages and link structures within these pages, we can gain a deeper understanding of the strategies employed by our competitors. This analysis provides us with valuable intelligence on the number and type of pages they utilize, as well as their internal linking practices, helping us refine our own approach to effectively compete in the search engine results.

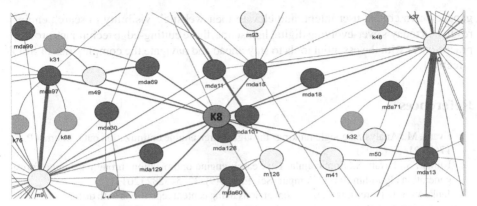

Fig. 7. Undirected Graph of KP.org and Competitors' Pages

In relation to the main breast cancer page, K8, within the KP.org domain, we have discovered the presence of 10 minor pages that are actively competing with it. Additionally, there is one PDF file that is also vying for visibility and engagement on the same topic. This competition among the various pages and the PDF file poses a challenge in effectively driving traffic to the K8 page.

6 Conclusion and Future Work

In conclusion, our study highlights the transformative impact of NLP and ML techniques within the domain of SEO. These technologies excel in deciphering the intricacies of natural language in search queries and web content, enhancing our understanding of user intent and content quality. Simultaneously, ML techniques play a pivotal role in dissecting quantitative factors such as keyword density, backlinks, and user engagement, all crucial for achieving higher search rankings. Building on this foundation, our research has presented a comprehensive and practical solution to address two fundamental SEO challenges: content optimization and the prevention of keyword cannibalization.

Looking ahead, our work identifies areas for future development and improvement. Our primary focus is on expanding our healthcare datasets, encompassing diverse data types such as clickstream data, page and query performance data, business Objectives and Key Results (OKR) data, and conversion data. By doing so, we aim to deepen our understanding of specific words and entities within the context of the healthcare domain. Additionally, we acknowledge the need for comprehensive performance testing and plan to integrate evaluations from various sources. We propose the implementation of a "voting" mechanism to accommodate the diverse metric priorities within our organization, which will allow us to track preferences over time and identify consistently successful teams or individuals. This iterative process is critical for bridging the gap between predicting future performance, reporting on actual performance, and minimizing disparities between the two.

In summary, the fusion of NLP and graph analysis in our research empowers SEO professionals to uncover opportunities for targeted keyword optimization, bridge content gaps, discern crucial user intent, and elevate their website's visibility in search engine results. In today's ever-evolving digital landscape, these cutting-edge techniques provide practitioners with the essential tools to stay ahead and navigate the complexities of SEO effectively.

References

1. Evans, M.: Analysing google rankings through search engine optimization data. Internet Res. **17**(1), 21–37 (2007)
2. Kumar, S., Pavan, S., Somayajula, K.: Search engine optimization through spanning forest generation algorithm. Int. J. Comput. Sci. Eng. **3**(9), 3275–3282 (2011)
3. Jankowski, J.: Increasing website conversions using content repetitions with different levels of persuasion. In: Selamat, A., Nguyen, N.T., Haron, H. (eds.) ACIIDS 2013. LNCS (LNAI), vol. 7803, pp. 439–448. Springer, Heidelberg (2013). https://doi.org/10.1007/978-3-642-36543-0_45
4. Agarwal, V.: 5 Search Engine Optimization Trends for 2017. The Next Web (TNW). Accessed 1 Nov (2017). https://thenextweb.com/insider/2017/01/11/5-search-engine-optimization-trends-for-2017/
5. Nayak, P.: How AI powers great search results (2022). https://blog.google/products/search/how-ai-powers-great-search-results/
6. Yuniarthe, Y.: Application of artificial intelligence (AI) in search engine optimization (SEO). In: International Conference on Soft Computing, Intelligent System and Information Technology (ICSIIT) (2017)
7. Godlevsky, M., Orekhov, S., Orekhova, E.: Theoretical fundamentals of search engine optimization based on machine learning. In: ICT in Education, Research and Industrial Applications. Integration, Harmonization and Knowledge Transfer, ICTERI (2017)
8. Salminen, J., Corporan, J., Marttila, R., Salenius, T., Jansen, B.: Using machine learning to predict ranking of webpages in the gift industry: factors for search-engine optimization. In: Proceedings of the 9th International Conference on Information Systems and Technologies (ICIST 2019), pp. 1–8 (2019)
9. Drivas, I., Sakas, D., Giannakopoulos, G., Kyriaki-Manessi, D.: Big data analytics for search engine optimization. Big Data Cogn. Comput. **4**(2), 5 (2020)
10. Portier, W., Li, Y., Adolphe, K.: Feature selection and classification methods for predicting search engine ranking. In: Proceedings of the 2020 3rd International Conference on Signal Processing and Machine Learning (SPML), pp. 84–90 (2020)
11. Vinutha, M.: Insights into search engine optimization using natural language processing and machine learning. Int. J. Adv. Comput. Sci. Appl. **14**(2), 86–96 (2023)
12. Reisenbichler, M., Reutterer, T., Schweidel, D., Dan, D.: Supporting content marketing with natural language generation. Mark. Sci. **41**(3), 441–452 (2022)
13. Jenkins, P., et al.: Natural language annotations for search engine optimization. In: Proceedings of the Web Conference 2020, pp. 2856–2862 (2020)
14. Sharma, S., Mahajan, S., Rana, V.: A semantic framework for ecommerce search engine optimization. Int. J. Inf. Technol. **11**(1), 31–36 (2018)
15. Horasan, F.: Keyword extraction for search engine optimization using latent semantic analysis. J. Polytech. **24**(2), 473–479 (2021)
16. Devlin, J., Chang, M., Lee, K., Toutanova, K.: BERT: pre-training of deep bidirectional transformers for language understanding. In: Proceedings of NAACL-HLT 2019, pp. 4171–4186 (2019)
17. BERTopic GitHub Homepage. https://github.com/MaartenGr/BERTopic

18. Grover, A., Leskovec, J.: node2vec: scalable feature learning for networks. In: Proceedings of the 22nd ACM SIGKDD International Conference on Knowledge Discovery and Data Mining, KDD 2016, pp. 855–864 (2016)
19. Power BI Homepage. https://powerbi.microsoft.com/en-us/
20. Pyspellchecker Homepage. https://pypi.org/project/pyspellchecker/

Evaluation of Integrated XAI Frameworks for Explaining Disease Prediction Models in Healthcare

Hong Qing Yu[(✉)] [iD], Adebola Alaba, and Ebere Eziefuna

University of Derby, Derby DE22 1GB, UK
h.yu@derby.ac.uk

Abstract. Explainable AI was created to solve the black box problems of deep learning models. Various explainable AI algorithms can highlight the features used by a black box model in deciding. Integrated frameworks were developed with multiple machine learning capabilities including model explanation. This research aims to investigate which of the integrated frameworks is more implementable within the healthcare sector and to evaluate how well the selected frameworks can explain prediction done with a tabular, natural language processing and image dataset. We investigated OmniXAI and InterpretML frameworks and the selected explainers are LIME and SHAP. Prostate cancer, pneumonia chest x-ray and medical question and answer were used as the datasets for tabular, image and natural language processing predictions. The feature importance score was used to compare and evaluate the explanations of the algorithms. Findings show that OmniXAI supports more methods and data formats. It can implement and explain tabular, image and NLP predictions while InterpretML supports only tabular data. InterpretML had a better plot of the explanation for the tabular prediction. InterpretML is more user-friendly and easily implementable. The OmniXAI integrated framework can be used in laboratories where tests are carried out with results stored in text, image, or CSV format. As the results are fed into the models for prediction, the explainers of the integrated frameworks will give insights into the model predictions. InterpretML can be implemented in laboratories where tabular results are been generated.

Keywords: Explainability AI · Machine Learning and Healthcare

1 Introduction

1.1 Background

Artificial Intelligence (AI) is being utilized to address various human problems in the world today. AI involves computational models that imitate human cognitive abilities [1, 11]. Through AI, a system can be taught from data and trained to think critically, learn from experience, and improve itself intuitively. AI has experienced several stages of evolution since its creation over six decades ago, and recent advancements in Big Data and large computing technology have given it an edge [8]. Artificial learners have

J. Qi and P. Yang (Eds.): IoTBDH 2023, CCIS 2019, pp. 14–28, 2024.
https://doi.org/10.1007/978-3-031-52216-1_2

achieved breakthroughs in various fields, including autonomous vehicles, weaponry, bioinformatics, and healthcare, with the goal of developing machines that can learn and think like humans. Businesses are actively investing in the research and development of advanced AI technologies, which heavily rely on the availability of data [2]. Autonomous disease detection has been made possible by Deep Learning (DL), a subfield of machine learning. This technology can replicate the human brain's ability to process language, recognize images and objects, develop drugs, diagnose illnesses, and make decisions. DL can effectively analyse data, including medical images [10]. AI technology has been successful in the healthcare industry, particularly in surgery and disease diagnostics. However, some AI models are difficult to understand, which makes it challenging for medical professionals to draw clinical conclusions that can be explained. To boost doctors' trust in medical AI applications, transparency is essential, and explainable artificial intelligence (XAI) is being studied to make applications more credible and incorporated into practice. As ML/DL algorithms become more complex, the demand for XAI is increasing. It helps users understand models' behaviour, which is just as important as their performance. XAI makes black-box models more transparent and intelligible in two ways: overall decision-making or specific result insights [4].

2 Literature Review

In 1993, Swartout and Moore made the first mention of the idea of interpreting AI systems followed by Van Lent, Fisher, and Mancuso in 2004. Contrary to the black-box nature of current AI systems, the term XAI was first used to characterise the internal workings of game simulations. Due to the rising use of AI/ML in daily life, the term XAI gained popularity. Pressure from society, ethics, and the law calls for a new generation of AI that can explain its internal workings and enable users to comprehend the reasoning process behind its judgments [14]. XAI can make AI systems more reliable, compliant, efficient, and resilient. XAI involves using techniques to create AI applications that end-users can comprehend and interpret. These users could be domain experts, data scientists, or even individuals without academic knowledge about AI. The popularity of DL and its use in real-world applications has spurred a desire to understand the reasoning behind its decisions. Generally, users prefer transparent AI models that are easy to interpret and explain. The breadth of XAI covers almost all application fields, from healthcare to agriculture [13]. When it comes to ML models, their understandability and believability are crucial factors in making them interpretable for the target audience. Explainability is the key to describing a phenomenon in a way that the audience can understand with ease. In the context of XAI, explainability refers to the AI's ability to provide users with a deeper understanding of the predictions obtained from a model, from a more methodological point of view [9].

2.1 XAI Explanation Methods

Local Explanation. Local explainability is crucial for clinicians using model predictions in treatment. It helps explain why a model made a certain prediction and can be included in clinical decision support software. Local explanations focus on individual cases. Techniques like LIME are commonly used for local explainability [16].

Global Explanation. To verify that a model is learning correctly, for instance, that the variables influencing model predictions are consistent with clinical knowledge, global explainability is crucial during the model-building process. The accuracy, fairness, or generalizability of a model may be affected by biases in the training data, which can be evaluated using global quality control methodologies. Additionally, there is increased interest in developing original scientific ideas employing global explanations [15].

Ante-Hoc. These are models that are naturally simple and interpretable such as decision trees, support vector machines and linear regression models. Their architecture and input format determine their output format. A common strategy for achieving interpretability through these inherently interpretable models is through rule sets, linear models, decision trees, case-based reasoning, and generalised additive algorithms. These algorithms produce outputs that are understandable by humans [14].

Post-Hoc. This method of explanation, also known as surrogate methods, analyses deep learning models like neural networks that have already been trained to gain an understanding of their inner workings. Then, they attempt to describe the behaviour of the resulting black box network. The explanations can be either local or global, as well as model-specific or model-agnostic. [3].

Model Agnostic. Model Agnostic: Rather than relying on modelling techniques, model-agnostic techniques work by recognising the association between input-output pairs of trained models. The underlying structural framework that is employed to determine the outcome is independent of the models. The flexible model methods, explanation approaches, and representation techniques are further categories for the model-agnostic models.

Model Specific. This mode of explanation is used for specific models. These explainers are built to explain the internal workings of a particular model or group of models. Such models are heavily reliant on a model's capabilities and attributes. To execute their tasks, model-specific algorithms inspect or provide detailed information about the model's internal workings.

2.2 XAI Explanation Algorithms

Shapley Additive Explanations. A method proposed by [12] involves the use of Shapley values to explain models. The Shapley Additive Explanations (SHAP) method uses game theory to determine how a specific input x is predicted by calculating the contribution of each feature toward that output prediction. The data features are treated as players in a coalition game, and Shapley values are used to ensure a fair distribution of payouts. Similar to LIME, data features in the SHAP method can be categorized in tabular data or groups of superpixels in images. The problem is formulated as a set of linear functions, where the explanation becomes a linear function of features [6]. This method provides a consistent way to interpret the results of any machine learning model and SHAP is effective in explaining both model-agnostic and model-specific situations.

Local Interpretable Model-Agnostic Explanations. Local Interpretable Model-Agnostic Explanations (LIME), estimate the given prediction of a model locally [12].

Being a feature-scoring method, LIME perturbs data input samples and assesses if predictions have changed to better understand the model. LIME analyses and classifies observations. It helps users understand model behaviour, including picture and tabular data classification. All models can be treated as black boxes with LIME's model independence [7].

2.3 Integrated XAI Frameworks

Omni Explainable Artificial Intelligence. OmniXAI is a new Python library that offers interpretive machine-learning techniques and explainable AI capabilities. It provides a range of explanation methods for different data types, models, and stages of the ML process. The library supports multiple data types, including tabular data, images, texts, and time series, and various explanation methods, including feature-attribution, counterfactual, and gradient-based explanations.

InterpretML. InterpretML is a Python library from Microsoft that offers interpretability techniques for machine learning. It provides two levels of interpretability for transparent and black box models, with a consistent interface and built-in visualization framework for easy comparison. The Explainable Boosting Machine is included, along with advanced ML techniques from Microsoft and third-party libraries. InterpretML enables users to gain a comprehensive understanding of their model's behaviour and debug predictions.

3 Research Methodology

This research will use machine learning to analyse data using quantitative methodology. It will involve preprocessing datasets for tabular, image, and natural language processing predictions, developing prediction models, and evaluating the explainability of predictions using LIME and SHAP. The models will be evaluated using the confusion matrix, accuracy, and precision while the explainer algorithms will be evaluated and compared using the feature importance score.

3.1 Dataset Description

The datasets used for this research are centred on prostate cancer, pneumonia, and medical question-and-answer datasets (MedQuAD). The prostate cancer dataset is used for the tabular data model prediction and explanation while the pneumonia dataset is used for image prediction. These datasets were obtained from Kaggle, a platform where users can work with other users, find, and publish datasets, use GPU-integrated notebooks, and compete with other data scientists to solve data science challenges.

3.2 Ethical Considerations

The research follows ethical norms and practices to ensure responsible and ethical use of data. This includes ensuring data privacy and confidentiality, transparency and reproducibility of the analytical process and model training, checking for fairness and bias in the dataset and machine learning processes, taking accurate measures to ensure the integrity and correctness of the output, and considering the broader implications on society, culture, and the environment.

3.3 Design of Experiment

This section gives insights into the intended approach for the omnixai integrated framework. Figure 1. is a pictorial representation of the experiment design.

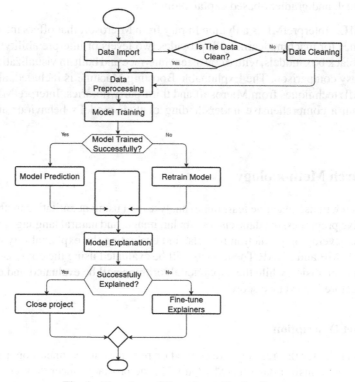

Fig. 1. Flowchart of Experiment Design Source

4   Results and Evaluation

4.1   Tabular Prediction and Explanation

The classifiers used for the model training were the Logistic Regression and Random Forest. The classifiers were able to classify all the instances in the test data. Both the actual and predictive positive instances (recall and precision) were predicted accurately by the models as shown in Table 1. The test data had a total of 20 instances with 12 of them having the Malignant diagnosis results while 8 had Benign. This performance is indicative that the models performed remarkably well on the dataset as indicated by [64].

Table 1. Model Results for Tabular Data.

ML Algorithm	Label	Accuracy	Precision	Support
Random Forest	0	1.00	1.00	12
	1	1.00	1.00	8
Logistic Regression	0	1.00	1.00	12
	1	1.00	1.00	8

Evaluation of Predicted Class 0 (Malignant). A prostate cell with a symmetry of 0.192, perimeter of 126, area of 1152, texture of 19, compactness of 0.127, fractal dimension of 0.060. radius of 10 and smoothness of 0.105 is predicted as Malignant by the logistic regression model which is an accurate prediction. Cell that has a larger size tend to be considered as Malignant. In addition to the digital rectal examination, PSA blood tests, other scans, and biopsy [5]. The OmniXAI LIME and SHAP explainers identified the perimeter attribute as the most important feature. As shown in Fig. 2, LIME assigned the feature an importance score of 0.022 while SHAP assigned an importance score of 0.31 as shown in Fig. 3. Next to the perimeter feature in the order of importance is the area feature. It had an importance score of 0.29 for SHAP and 0.018. The fractal dimension, radius, symmetry, and smoothness features are less important for this prediction. The features were sorted in descending order of importance for the SHAP explainer. This makes it easier to read and comprehend compared to LIME's plot. All features positively influenced the prediction of the models. The plot of explainability for InterpretML as shown in Fig. 4 slightly differs from OmniXAI, a prostate cell with a symmetry of 0.16, perimeter of 129, area of 1132, texture of 14, compactness of 0.18, fractal dimension of 0.07, radius of 20 and smoothness of 0.12 is predicted as Malignant by the linear regression model which is an accurate prediction. The LIME Explainer of InterpretML identified perimeter as the feature with the least influence while area has the most influence in the prediction of the model. The explain-ability plot of InterpretML is better than the plot of OmniXAI. The feature importance scores can be seen and read properly. This can easily be understood by users.

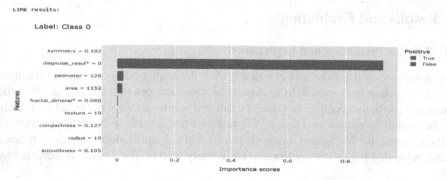

Fig. 2. OmniXAI LIME Explanation for a Predicted Malignant Instance.

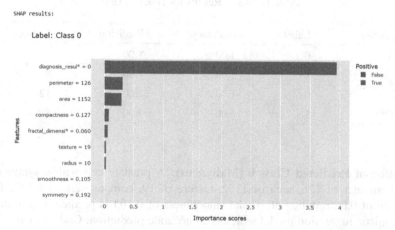

Fig. 3. OmniXAI SHAP Explanation for a Predicted Malignant Instance.

Evaluation of Predicted Class 1 (Benign). A prostate cell with a symmetry of 0.139, perimeter of 85, area of 552, texture of 14, compactness of 0.051, radius of 14 and smoothness of 0.074 is predicted as Benign by the logistic regression model. The OmniXAI LIME and SHAP explainers identified the compactness attribute as the most important feature for this prediction. As shown in Fig. 5, LIME assigned the feature an importance score of 0.02 while SHAP assigned an importance score of 0.34 as shown in Fig. 6. For LIME, the next important feature after compactness is the area with an importance score of 0.006 while the SHAP importance score for area is 0.095. For SHAP, the next important feature after compactness is the perimeter with an importance score of 0.12 while the LIME importance score for the perimeter is 0.0058. The fractal dimension, radius, symmetry, and smoothness features respectively impacted the predictions negatively. For InterpretML, the logistic regression model predicted a prostate cell with a symmetry of 0.17, perimeter of 95, area of 663, texture of 27, compactness of 0.09, radius of 23 and smoothness of 0.09 as Benign. The LIME Explainer of InterpretML identified perimeter as the feature with the least influence while area has the most influence in the prediction of the model as shown in Fig. 7.

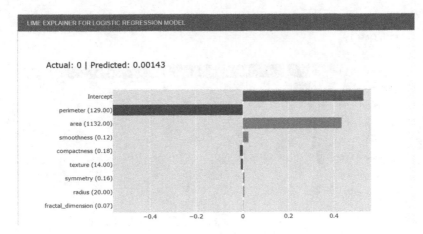

Fig. 4. InterpretML LIME Explanation for a Predicted Malignant Instance.

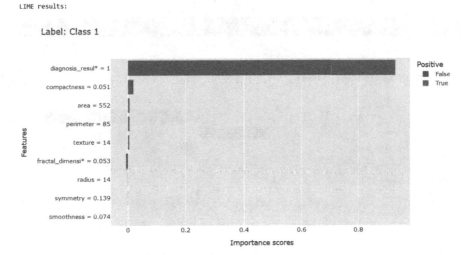

Fig. 5. OmniXAI LIME Explanation for a Predicted Benign Instance.

4.2 Natural Language Processing Prediction & Explanation

The text for the NLP prediction was selected from the MedQuAD dataset. The selection was based on the Breast Cancer and Prostate Cancer focus areas. Two different models were used, the Random Forest Classifier Model and the distilbert-base-uncased-finetuned-sst-2-english pre-trained model which is based on the DistilBERT architecture and implemented in the transformer library. The pre-trained model was used because SHAP explainers for NLP tasks can only support the text classification pipeline from the transformer model. The LIME explainer was used to explain the predictions of the

SHAP results:

Label: Class 1

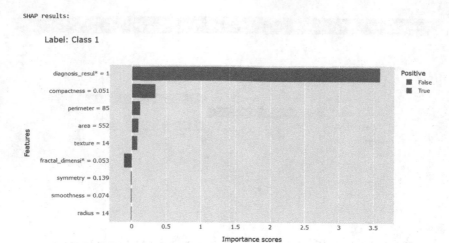

Fig. 6. OmniXAI SHAP Explanation for a Predicted Benign Instance.

LIME EXPLAINER FOR LOGISTIC REGRESSION MODEL

Actual: 1 | Predicted: 0.0894

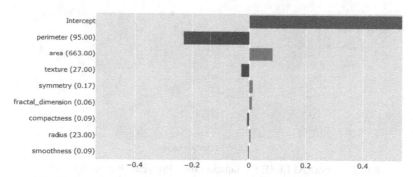

Fig. 7. InterpretML LIME Explanation for a Predicted Benign Instance

random forest model while SHAP was used to explain the sentiment analysis done by the distilbert pre-trained model.

OmniXAI LIME Explainer. The random forest classifier model built had an accuracy of 95%. This means that the model was able to correctly predict 95% of the instances available in the dataset. According to the confusion matrix report as shown in Table 2, the model was able to 10 of the texts for the positive class accurately while two were wrongly classified as negative. LIME was used to explain the predictions made by the random forest model. Figures 8 and 9 show the explanation generated by OmniXAI LIME Explainer. In Fig. 8, the model predicted that the phrase is affiliated with prostate cancer. The LIME explainer was able to identify words such as prostate, men and semen were key in classifying text instances as prostate cancer. In Fig. 9, the model predicted that the phrase is affiliated with breast cancer. LIME explained that words such as breast, women, chest, and nodes are key in classifying the text instance as breast cancer.

Table 2. Confusion Matrix Report for Random Forest NLP Model

	Actual Positive Class	Actual Negative Class
Predicted Positive Class (True)	10	0
Predicted Negative Class (False)	2	8

Instance 0: Class Prostate Cancer
prostate men called be semen sexual urine symptoms bladder is

Fig. 8. OmniXAI LIME Explanation for a Predicted Prostate Cancer Instance.

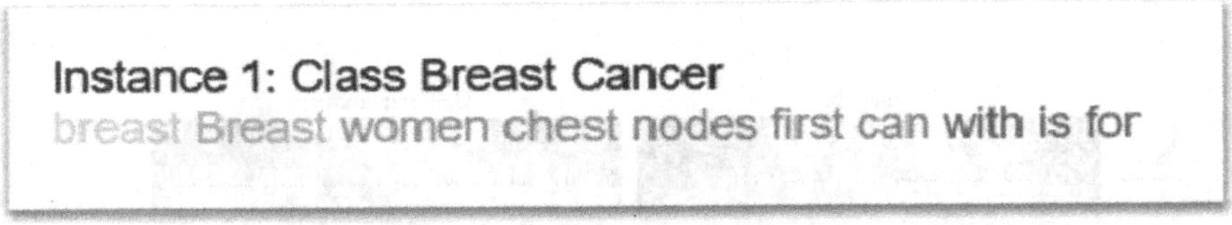

Instance 1: Class Breast Cancer
breast Breast women chest nodes first can with is for

Fig. 9. OmniXAI LIME Explanation for a Predicted Breast Cancer Instance.

OmniXAI SHAP Explainer. The SHAP explainer was used to explain the prediction of the DistilBERT model. The pre-trained model was used because SHAP explainers for NLP tasks can only support the text classification pipeline from the transformer model. SHAP was supplied with an omnixai text object that contained some questions and answers relating to prostate cancer and breast cancer. However, SHAP explained how the instances of the omnixai text objects were classified as either negative or positive by the transformer model. For instance, the MedQuAD answer instance in Fig. 11 was classified as negative using the phrases "not know how to prevent g lau com a", "risk groups for the disease" and words such as "loss", "cancer", "glaucoma" and "dilated" while the word "prevent" greatly influenced the classification of the text instance as negative in Fig. 10.

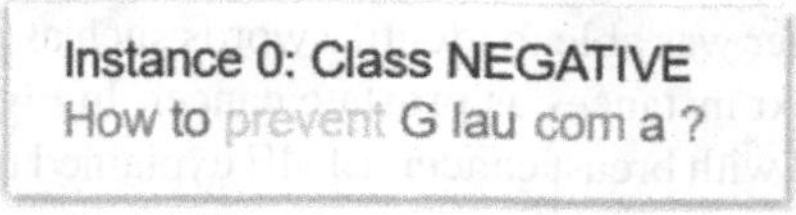

Instance 0: Class NEGATIVE
How to prevent G lau com a ?

Fig. 10. OmniXAI SHAP Explanation for a MedQuAD Question Classification.

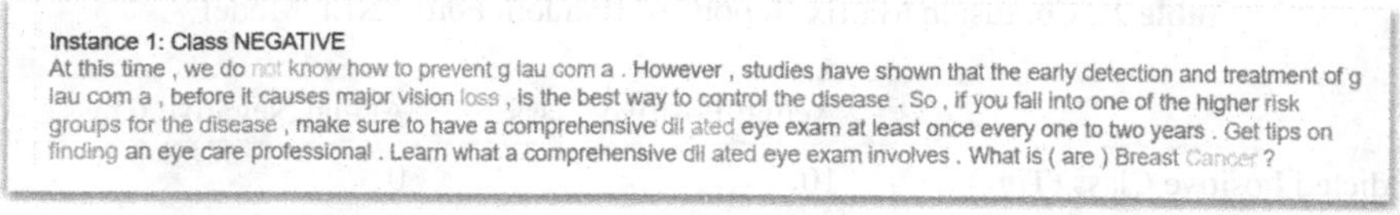

Instance 1: Class NEGATIVE
At this time , we do not know how to prevent g lau com a . However , studies have shown that the early detection and treatment of g lau com a , before it causes major vision loss , is the best way to control the disease . So , if you fall into one of the higher risk groups for the disease , make sure to have a comprehensive dil ated eye exam at least once every one to two years . Get tips on finding an eye care professional . Learn what a comprehensive dil ated eye exam involves . What is (are) Breast Cancer ?

Fig. 11. OmniXAI SHAP Explanation for a MedQuAD Answer Classification.

4.3 Image Prediction and Explanation

We implemented a CNN-based chest disease classification model with 93.98% training accuracy and 88.14% validation accuracy. Now we tried to apply OmniXAI LIME and SHAP methods to explain the prediction results. LIME segments images into patches, constructing weighted local models through permuted instances with changes visible in grey. Input images with grey backings in Fig. 12 shows LIME's segmentation. LIME identified the relevant as well as irrelevant region in this instance. SHAP utilises Shapley values, averaging feature contributions, visualising red and blue pixel impacts (see Fig. 13).

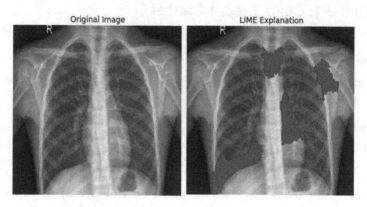

Original Image   LIME Explanation

Fig. 12. Explanation using OmniXAI LIME

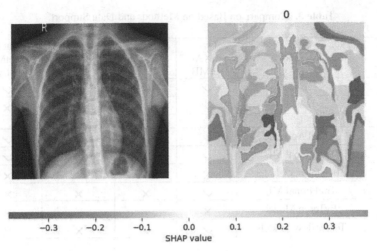

Fig. 13. Explanation using OmniXAI SHAP

5   Discussion

OmniXAI offers explainers for various data formats and has a DataAnalyzer feature for exploratory data analysis. The GitHub tutorial is helpful for implementation, but there are limited resources for bug fixes and problem resolution. Tabular and NLP prediction require preprocessing, and LIME and SHAP explainers can be used for visualization. Image prediction is more difficult and may encounter issues with the explainers. InterpretML also has a GitHub repository, and it supports tabular data for black box prediction. It only requires installation of the interpret package and can visualize model performance using ROC curves. LimeTabular creates LIME explanations and ShapKernel creates SHAP explanations, but the SHAP explanation plot failed to generate. InterpretML also has a dashboard feature, but it is not yet supported in cloud environments. Two integrated frameworks were compared based on tasks and methods used during implementation and user experience metrics. OmniXAI is better for tasks and methods (see Table 3), while InterpretML is better for user experience (see Table 4). Both frameworks can be used in healthcare organizations to execute necessary processes end to end and provide clinicians with insights into model predictions. OmniXAI is suited for labs with test results in various formats, while InterpretML can be used for tabular results.

Table 3. Comparison Based on Methods and Data Support.

Task	Method	Om- niXAI LIME	OmniXAI SHAP	InterpretML LIME	Inter- pretML SHAP
Data Sup- port	Tabular	✓	✓	✓	✓
	Image	✓	✓	✗	✗
	NLP				
Tabu- lar	Model Agnostic	✓	✓	✓	✓
	Traditional ML	✓	✓	✓	✓
NLP	Transformer Model	✗	✓	✗	✗
	Traditional ML	✓	✗	✗	✗
Image	PyTorch Model	✗	✓	✗	✗
	Tensorflow Models	✓	✓	✗	✗

Table 4. Comparison Based on User Experience

Metric	Description	OmniXAI	InterpretML
Fidelity	Do the explanations accurately represent the model outputs?	Yes	Yes
Consistency	Are the explanations consistent across different instances?	Yes	Yes
Ease of Use	Is the integrated framework easy to implement and straight forward?	No	Yes
Quality of Visualization	How effective is the Visualization of the explanations?	Less Effective	Very Effective
User-Friendliness	How easy is it to interact with the explanation visualization	Static Plot, No interaction	Dynamic Plot, Easy Interaction
Community Support	Does the integrated framework have a community of helpers, tutorials, and documentation	No Community. Tutorials and documentation are available on GitHub	No Community. Tutorials and documentation are available on GitHub

6 Conclusion

The goal of this research is to investigate how integrated frameworks explain disease prediction models in healthcare. This research carried out an empirical study to identify and preprocess datasets for tabular, image, and natural language processing predictions. Develop prediction models and use explainers in XAI frameworks to explain the model outputs and evaluate the explanation using feature importance scores. The selected frameworks for this research are OmniXAI and InterpretML. As discussed in Sect. 5, OmniXAI supports more data types and methods than InterpretML. Based on user experience metrics, InterpretML is the better integrated framework. Although both integrated frameworks have no community help, they have proven to be very useful in the healthcare sector. OmniXAI integrated frameworks in laboratories can provide clinicians with insights into model predictions. These frameworks can be used for testing outcomes in text or tabular format, combining the clinicians' intelligence and experience for accurate diagnosis. InterpretML is also suitable for laboratories generating tabular results.

References

1. Abacha, A.B., Demner-Fushman, D.: A question-entailment approach to question answering. BMC Bioinform. **20**(1) (2019). https://doi.org/10.1186/s12859-019-3119-4
2. Adadi, A.: A survey on data-efficient algorithms in big data era. J. Big Data **8**(1), 1–54 (2021). https://doi.org/10.1186/s40537-021-00419-9
3. Alicioglu, G., Sun, B.: A survey of visual analytics for explainable artificial intelligence methods. Comput. Graphics (Pergamon) **102,** 502–520 (2022). https://doi.org/10.1016/j.cag.2021.09.002
4. Cancer Research UK: Examination of your prostate (2023). https://www.cancerresearchuk.org/about-cancer/tests-and-scans/examination-prostate
5. Celik, S.: Prostate cancer analysis with ML methods (2020). https://www.kaggle.com/code/sadielik/prostate-cancer-analysis-with-ml-methods
6. Deshpande, N.M., et al.: Explainable artificial intelligence–a new step towards the trust in medical diagnosis with AI frameworks: a review. CMES - Comput. Model. Eng. Sci., 843–872 (2022). https://doi.org/10.32604/cmes.2022.021225
7. Duan, Y., Edwards, J.S., Dwivedi, Y.K.: Artificial intelligence for decision making in the era of Big Data – evolution, challenges and research agenda. Int. J. Inf. Manage. **48**, 63–71 (2019). https://doi.org/10.1016/j.ijinfomgt.2019.01.021
8. Durán, J.M., Jongsma, K.R.: Who is afraid of black box algorithms? On the epistemological and ethical basis of trust in medical AI. J. Med. Ethics **47**(5), 329–335 (2021). https://doi.org/10.1136/medethics-2020-106820
9. Hatherley, J., Sparrow, R. and Howard, M. (2022) 'The Virtues of Interpretable Medical Artificial Intelligence', Cambridge Quarterly of Healthcare Ethics, pp. 1–10. Available at: https://doi.org/10.1017/s0963180122000305
10. ICO: guide to the general data protection regulation (GDPR) (2022)
11. Janssen, J.H.N.: The right to explanation: means for 'white-boxing' the black-box? (2019)
12. Mcleod, S.: Correlation in statistics: meaning, types, examples & coefficient (2023). https://www.simplypsychology.org/correlation.html
13. Minh, D., et al.: Explainable artificial intelligence: a comprehensive review. Artif. Intell. Rev. **55**(5), 3503–3568 (2022). https://doi.org/10.1007/s10462-021-10088-y

14. Muddamsetty, S.M., Jahromi, M.N.S. Moeslund, T.B.: Expert level evaluations for explainable AI (XAI) methods in the medical domain (2020). https://www.researchgate.net/publication/346084953

15. Ordish, J. Hall, A.: Black box Medicine and Transparency: Machine Learning Landscape (2020). www.phgfoundation.org

16. Poon, A.I.F., Sung, J.J.Y.: Opening the black box of AI-medicine. J. Gastroenterol. Hepatol. **36**(3), 581–584 (2021). https://doi.org/10.1111/jgh.15384

Zero-Shot Medical Information Retrieval via Knowledge Graph Embedding

Yuqi Wang[1,3], Zeqiang Wang[1], Wei Wang[1]([✉])(iD), Qi Chen[1], Kaizhu Huang[2](iD), Anh Nguyen[3](iD), and Suparna De[4](iD)

[1] Xi'an Jiaotong-Liverpool University, Suzhou, China
{yuqi.wang17,zeqiang.wang22}@student.xjtlu.edu.cn,
{wei.wang03,qi.chen02}@xjtlu.edu.cn
[2] Duke Kunshan University, Kunshan, China
kaizhu.huang@dukekunshan.edu.cn
[3] University of Liverpool, Liverpool, UK
anh.nguyen@liverpool.ac.uk
[4] University of Surrey, Surrey, UK
s.de@surrey.ac.uk

Abstract. In the era of the Internet of Things (IoT), the retrieval of relevant medical information has become essential for efficient clinical decision-making. This paper introduces MedFusionRank, a novel approach to zero-shot medical information retrieval (MIR) that combines the strengths of pre-trained language models and statistical methods while addressing their limitations. The proposed approach leverages a pre-trained BERT-style model to extract compact yet informative keywords. These keywords are then enriched with domain knowledge by linking them to conceptual entities within a medical knowledge graph. Experimental evaluations on medical datasets demonstrate MedFusionRank's superior performance over existing methods, with promising results with a variety of evaluation metrics. MedFusionRank demonstrates efficacy in retrieving relevant information, even from short or single-term queries.

Keywords: medical information retrieval · Internet of Things · natural language processing · clinical decision-making · medical knowledge graph

1 Introduction

The widespread adoption of the Internet of Things (IoT) has enabled the collection of large amounts of medical text data. By using IoT to identify patients, transfer information to central databases, and search for relevant medical texts such as electronic health records (EHRs) and disease-related papers, we can improve the efficiency of treatment procedures and therapeutic outcomes [8,19]. For instance, the MIMIC-III [12] and MIMIC-IV [11] critical care medical databases use IoT systems to collect structured clinical data and texts. These

© The Author(s), under exclusive license to Springer Nature Switzerland AG 2024
J. Qi and P. Yang (Eds.): IoTBDH 2023, CCIS 2019, pp. 29–40, 2024.
https://doi.org/10.1007/978-3-031-52216-1_3

medical texts have become the foundation for medical natural language processing, serving as corpora for pre-training large language models and embeddings [1,16,32]. Additionally, the use of IoT in healthcare has the potential to revolutionise patient care by providing real-time monitoring and personalised treatment plans based on individual patient data. This can lead to improved patient outcomes and reduced healthcare costs [7].

A key challenge in healthcare is enabling real-time, personalised clinical decision-making beyond traditional tasks like diagnostic classification and outcome prediction. Effective clinical decision support fundamentally relies on the ability to retrieve relevant information from massive amounts of unstructured EHR data. While earlier work in medical information retrieval relied on statistical methods like BM25 [23] with Term Frequency-Inverse Document Frequency (TF-IDF) features, these techniques struggled with the complexity and sparsity of medical text. Medical notes exhibit pervasive synonym phenomena, with different terms like "hypertension" and "high blood pressure" denoting identical concepts. Abbreviations and shorthand introductions are also ubiquitous, posing difficulties for simple lexical matching.

Recently, pre-trained large language models (LLMs) like BERT [6], Alpaca [27], and Llama [29] have shown promise by learning generalisable representations of medical language. However, their computational overhead makes deployment directly onto resource-constrained IoT devices impractical. Training with massive LLMs requires substantial data, computing power, and memory exceeding the available on-device. Therefore, an open challenge is adapting the strengths of LLMs for medical search on embedded IoT systems. More efficient methods are needed to extract knowledge from LLMs and make it accessible for medical information retrieval on hardware-friendly architectures.

To address the aforementioned challenges, we propose a novel zero-shot information retrieval approach that integrates the strengths of statistical methods and pre-trained LLMs while mitigating their limitations. Our key insight is to leverage a pre-trained BERT-style model to extract compact yet informative keywords. These keywords are then enriched with domain knowledge by linking them to conceptual entities within a medical knowledge graph. Our method has demonstrated promising results on two benchmark datasets, outperforming a range of existing Information Retrieval models across various evaluation metrics.

2   Related Work

Medical information retrieval (MIR) aims to retrieve relevant medical data from sources such as EHR. However, it faces distinct challenges that extend beyond conventional information retrieval (IR) - complex medical terminology, heterogeneous data, privacy constraints, and difficulties in system evaluation. While leveraging core IR techniques, MIR has specific requirements arising from the medical domain. In this section, we provide an overview of key IR methods that facilitate effective MIR.

2.1 Statistical Information Retrieval

Statistical information retrieval (Statistical IR) is a foundational approach that leverages probabilistic and statistical models to quantify the relevance of documents to user queries. This allows ranking search results by estimated relevance based on mathematical models. Popular statistical IR techniques, including vector space model [3], probabilistic retrieval model [25], and Okapi BM25 [23] rely heavily on weighted keyword matching between query and document terms. They estimate relevance using statistical signals like TF-IDF, and length normalisation. While very effective for many search tasks, these lexical similarity models have limitations. Specifically, they cannot account for semantic matching, failing to recognise synonyms and antonyms.

2.2 Neural Information Retrieval

Neural information retrieval (Neural IR) is a modern paradigm that leverages neural networks and deep learning techniques to overcome the limitations of statistical IR models. Neural IR models can be classified into two main types: first-stage retrieval methods and re-ranking methods.

First-Stage Methods. First-stage methods aim to directly retrieve relevant documents from a large collection using neural networks. These methods can be further categorised into sparse retrieval methods and dense retrieval methods. Sparse retrieval methods use sparse word representations, such as bag-of-words or TF-IDF, as inputs to neural networks and learn to rank documents based on their similarity to queries [5,15]. Dense retrieval methods, on the other hand, use dense vector representations, such as word embeddings or contextual embeddings, as inputs to neural networks and learn to map queries and documents into a common semantic space where their relevance can be measured by distance metrics [10,14,24].

Re-ranking Methods. Re-ranking methods use neural networks to refine the initial ranking results produced by a base retriever, such as BM25 or a sparse/dense retriever. These methods can be categorised into two main approaches: 1)Re-ranking with sentence embeddings: These methods treat each document independently as an instance and learn to score its relevance to the query [22]. They derive vector representations for the query and each document in a separate manner, compare their embeddings and assign relevance scores. 2) Re-ranking using a cross-encoder: These methods consider each query-document pair as an instance and learn to compare their relative relevance [31]. The cross-encoder jointly models the query and document to capture semantic matching.

3 Methodology

We show the overall architecture of our proposed method in Fig. 1. Specifically, it first extracts keywords from medical documents to capture semantic context. Then, medical embeddings for each keyword are constructed based on the

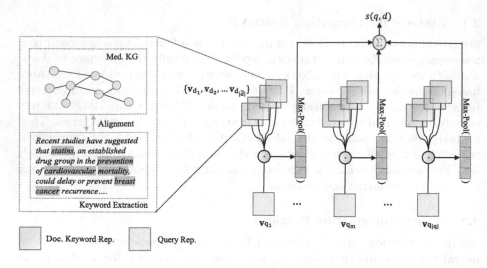

Fig. 1. The overall architecture of our proposed method.

domain-specific knowledge graph. The query and document keywords are compared in the medical embedding space and their similarity scores are aggregated to identify relevant information across query terms for retrieval.

3.1 Document Keyword Extraction

Given the inherent complexity of documents within the medical domain, often encompassing multiple aspects, the necessity of pre-processing before conducting IR becomes evident. One such approach involves the extraction of keywords that aptly describe and summarise the content. By utilising a contextualised attention-based pre-trained language model, the contextual information can be effectively harnessed to discern the document's relatively significant sections. Therefore, we utilise the RoBERTa [18] model for the initial encoding of the corpus documents. RoBERTa is a state-of-the-art language model that has demonstrated exceptional performance in various natural language processing tasks. Specifically, when dealing with a document d comprised of k words, denoted as $d = \{d_1, ...d_k\}$, we leverage the RoBERTa encoding function, $f(\cdot; \theta)$, to transform all the words into a coherent and meaningful semantic space, i.e.

$$\{\mathbf{h}_{<s>}, \mathbf{h}_{d_1}, ...\mathbf{h}_{d_k}, \mathbf{h}_{</s>}\} = f(\{<s>, d_1, ...d_k, </s>\}; \theta) \qquad (1)$$

where $\mathbf{h}_{d_i}$ is the representation of the i-th word in RoBERTa embedding space. $<s>$ and $</s>$ are two special tokens indicating the start and the end positions in the document, respectively. This process enables us to capture the intricate contextual relationships and nuances present within the document.

The comprehensive essence of the document is commonly encapsulated within the hidden state of the special token $<s>$; in order to estimate the significance of individual words within the document, we compute the cosine similarity between the representation of the special token $< s >$ and the representation of each word. We take the top K ranking words based on their similarity scores, and extract those as the key keywords for the document d. This process is articulated as follows:

$$\tilde{d} = \underset{d_i \in d}{\text{top}\, K} \left[\text{Sim} \left(\mathbf{h}_{d_i}, \mathbf{h}_{<s>} \right) \right] \tag{2}$$

where $\tilde{d}$ is the keyword set for document d, $\text{Sim}(\cdot)$ is the cosine similarity function. Based on our observation, the top 20 keywords can effectively capture the core semantic content of a document. Hence, we set the number of extracted keywords (K) to 20.

3.2   Medical Embedding Construction

In our work, the challenge posed by zero-shot IR is significant, primarily due to the absence of any prior exposure of the model to the medical domain. In this case, a crucial approach involves enhancing each keyword in the keyword set $\tilde{d}$ with relevant background information. This enrichment encompasses additional context, definitions, and pertinent details sourced from the medical field. In this endeavour, the Medical Subject Headings (MeSH) [17] knowledge graph emerges as an exceptional resource. MeSH is a meticulously structured and high-quality knowledge graph that encompasses a vast spectrum of medical concepts along with their relationships. For instance, the relation "*treatment*" connects the two concepts "*cancer*" and "*chemotherapy*". This indicates that chemotherapy is a type of treatment commonly used for cancer patients.

To harness the knowledge from MeSH, a method called Node2Vec [9] can be used to generate medical embeddings. The main idea is to treat this graph as a network, where nodes are concepts and edges represent relationships between concepts [32]. This method utilises random walks and learns latent representations of nodes that maximise the probability of the sampled walks. The objective function J for constructing the medical embeddings can be written as follows:

$$J = \max \left[\frac{1}{T} \sum_{i=1}^{T} \sum_{v_j \in \mathcal{C}(v_i)} \log p\left(v_j \mid v_i \right) \right] \tag{3}$$

where T is the number of the MeSH concepts and $\mathcal{C}(v_i)$ is a set containing surrounding words of v_i based on random walks in the knowledge graph. For this study, alignment between the keyword set $\tilde{d}$, the query q, and concepts in the MeSH knowledge graph were performed by matching keywords with concept names. This simple lexical approach to entity linking was chosen for its simplicity. However, it has known limitations, such as ambiguity and lack of semantic matching. Future work should explore more sophisticated techniques to deal with the issue.

3.3 Retrieval with Medical Knowledge

By acquiring all the medical embeddings for document keywords from a corpus in the MeSH knowledge graph embedding space through an offline process, we can retrieve relevant information for each word from a given human-generated query in an efficient manner. In particular, each query term can focus on each word in the document to identify the most relevant information in the document that can be retrieved by that specific query word. We aggregate all the relevance scores for each query term during the retrieval process, i.e.

$$s(q, d) = \sum_{i=1}^{|q|} \max_{j=1}^{|\tilde{d}|} \left[\mathbf{v}_{q_i} \odot \mathbf{v}_{d_j} \right] \tag{4}$$

where $|q|$ and $|\tilde{d}|$ are the number of words in the query and document keyword set, respectively. $\odot$ is the dot product operation symbol. $\mathbf{v}_{q_i}$ and $\mathbf{v}_{d_j}$ are corresponding medical embeddings for the i-th word in the query and j-th word in the document keyword set.

One clear limitation of Retrieval with Medical Knowledge is the equal weighting given to documents whose keyword sets contain query terms, regardless of term frequency. Despite the inclusion of background knowledge corresponding to each word in the document's keywords, factors such as term frequency should also be considered. BM25 [23] is a commonly used unsupervised ranking function, incorporating lexical aspects and statistical information to improve scoring. Leveraging medical embeddings enables the retrieval of candidate-relevant documents while applying BM25, which can further refine the ranking of those initial results by incorporating term frequency statistics. Therefore, we propose fusing the scores yielded by both approaches to improve overall performance, i.e.

$$\hat{s}(q, d) = \begin{cases} s(q, d) + s'(q, d) & \exists s'(q, d) \\ s(q, d) & \nexists s'(q, d) \end{cases} \tag{5}$$

where $s'(q, d)$ represents the BM25 score assigned to a given query q and document d. $\hat{s}(q, d)$ is the final score after the fusion.

4 Results and Evaluation

We evaluated the performance of our proposed models on two medical datasets: NFCorpus [2] and SCIFACT [30]. Both focus on retrieving medical abstracts relevant to search queries. The abstracts are written in technical medical terminology, mostly from PubMed. For each dataset, a range of metrics, including Mean Reciprocal Rank (MRR), Precision, normalised Discounted Cumulative Gain (nDCG), Precision (P) and Recall (R), was employed for a thorough evaluation. Our model was compared against several first-stage retrievers and BM25-based re-rankers to assess its effectiveness.

4.1   Baseline Models

First-Stage Retrievers

- **BioLinkBERT** [13] and **S-BERT** [22]: These are two BERT-based models that generate sentence embeddings using siamese networks. While S-BERT was pre-trained on a general domain question-answering dataset to create universal semantic embeddings, BioLinkBERT utilises contrastive learning on medical texts from PubMed to produce embeddings specialised for the medical domain.
- **DocT5Query** [20]: It leverages a pre-trained T5 [21] model to generate synthetic queries based on the document for text enrichment before indexing.
- **DeepCT** [4]: It employs the BERT model to estimate the weight of each word in the context of the document. These BERT-derived weights are then used to modify the term frequencies of the words.
- **BM25** [23]: It is a traditional unsupervised ranking function. The basic idea is that a more relevant document will contain more of the query terms, and multiple occurrences of a term can indicate higher relevance.

BM25-Based Re-Rankers

- **S-BERT** [22]: We used the same S-BERT model as described previously to re-rank the top 100 candidate documents retrieved in the first-stage for each query.
- **Cross Encoder** [31]: It passes both the query and document sentence simultaneously to a Transformer network, producing an output value between 0 and 1, which indicates the relevance of the sentence pair. In reference to a study by Thakur *et al.*[28], it is highlighted that MiniLM demonstrates the best performance. Therefore, we evaluate the performance when using MiniLM as the Cross Encoder for re-ranking.

4.2   Main Results

The main retrieval results are illustrated in Table 1. It demonstrates that BM25 is an effective baseline for zero-shot IR compared with bi-encoders such as S-BERT and BioLinkBERT. BM25 ranking alone achieves reasonable performance, which can be further improved by re-ranking using a cross-encoder model. This two-stage ranking pipeline achieves the best MRR results on the NFCorpus dataset. However, re-ranking based on BM25 has limitations stemming from BM25's dependence on exact term matching, which can cause relevant documents to be excluded from consideration during later re-ranking stages.

A noteworthy scenario emerged where the precision of MedRetriever at the top 1000 exhibited favourable results among all the baseline retrievers. In contrast, the nDCG at the top 10 demonstrated comparatively suboptimal performance. This disparity between precision and nDCG metrics suggests that although the MedRetriever is capable of retrieving a fair proportion of relevant

Table 1. Performances of first-stage retrievers, BM25-based re-rankers and our proposed models. †The results were cited from [28]. *MedRetriever refers to our proposed method as a standalone approach, distinct from its fusion with BM25.

Method	NFCorpus				SCIFACT			
	MRR	P@10	nDCG@10	R@1k	MRR	P@10	nDCG@10	R@1k
First-stage Retrievers								
BioLinkBERT	0.329	0.132	0.173	0.532	0.519	0.076	0.550	0.979
S-BERT	0.501	0.218	0.300	0.574	0.570	0.082	0.596	0.959
DocT5Query†	–	–	0.328	–	–	–	0.675	–
DeepCT†	–	–	0.283	–	–	–	0.630	–
BM25	0.537	0.233	0.325	0.372	0.635	0.088	0.665	0.980
BM25-based Re-rankers								
Cross Encoder	**0.591**	0.244	0.350	0.250	0.662	0.091	0.688	0.908
S-BERT	0.430	0.170	0.232	0.229	0.539	0.081	0.568	0.864
Our Proposed Models								
MedRetriever *	0.499	0.222	0.298	**0.644**	0.540	0.083	0.581	**0.990**
MedFusionRank	0.552	**0.262**	**0.357**	**0.644**	**0.673**	**0.094**	**0.705**	**0.990**

documents overall, it struggles to rank the most relevant documents at the very top of the list. When we combine scores from two methods, MedRetriever and BM25, the results consistently outperformed nearly all of the baseline methods across all evaluation metrics.

4.3   Out-of-Vocabulary Strategy

Table 2. Performances of using different out-of-vocabulary strategies for MedFusionRank

Method	NFCorpus				SCIFACT			
	MRR	P@10	nDCG@10	R@1k	MRR	P@10	nDCG@10	R@1k
Prefix Approx	0.552	0.262	0.357	**0.644**	0.673	0.094	0.705	0.990
CharLSTM	**0.553**	**0.263**	**0.358**	0.643	**0.684**	0.094	**0.713**	0.990

To handle out-of-vocabulary (OOV) words, this work incorporates two strategies: Prefix Approximation and a Character-level Long Short-Term Memory network (CharLSTM). Prefix Approximation, originally proposed in [26], identifies the longest common prefix between an OOV word and in-vocabulary words, then averages all embeddings sharing that prefix to represent the OOV term. On the other hand, the CharLSTM learns sequential character-level features of in-vocabulary words to construct a non-linear mapping from character sequences to medical embeddings. As depicted in Table 2, the CharLSTM achieves better overall performance compared to Prefix Approximation. This indicates that modelling the sequential patterns and characters of medical terminology plays a more vital role in estimating representations for OOV words in this domain.

4.4   Case Study

Table 3. Keywords in the retrieved document based on a single term as query

Query	Keywords in retrieved document				
zoloft	depression	depressive	antidepressants	exercise	sertraline
	aerobic	therapy	anxiety	treatment	medication
	therapeutic	50	disorders	mental	older
	effects	67	rating	mdd	diagnostic
myelopathy	spinal	sclerotic	paraplegia	cobalamin	spine
	vegetarian	vegan	subacute	cervical	vitamin
	degeneration	hypertonia	diagnosed	reflexia	impairment
	paresthesias	rehabilitative	hypotrophy	neurogenic	diet

To further evaluate the performance of our proposed model, we conducted a case study using short, single-term queries common in human searches. Statistical matching models like BM25 often struggle with these sparse queries, as the single terms may not exist in the corpus. As shown in Table 3, the sample query terms "*zoloft*" and "*myelopathy*" did not appear in any documents. However, our proposed model successfully retrieved relevant documents with medical concepts from the knowledge graph, ranking pertinent documents in the top 10 results for both queries.

In the first example, "*zoloft*" is an antidepressant medication. Therefore, "*depression*", "*depressive*", and "*anxiety*" are closely connected to "*zoloft*" since the medication aims to alleviate the symptoms associated with these conditions. In another example, "*myelopathy*" is a spinal cord pathology that can result from vitamin deficiency, spinal degeneration, or cord compression. The keywords "*spinal*", "*spine*", "*vitamin*" and "*degeneration*" from the retrieved document could be relevant to the query.

This case study highlights the potential of our proposed model to improve the search relevancy of short user queries. Our model effectively utilised associated medical concepts to match user information needs.

5   Conclusion and Future Work

In this paper, we have presented MedFusionRank, a novel zero-shot MIR approach that integrates the strengths of statistical methods and pre-trained language models. Our key insight is to leverage a pre-trained BERT-style model to extract compact yet informative keywords. These keywords are then enriched with domain knowledge by linking them to conceptual entities within a medical knowledge graph.

Our experiments on two benchmark medical datasets demonstrate that Med-FusionRank achieves promising results, outperforming a range of existing models across various evaluation metrics. The case study also reveals MedFusionRank's ability to retrieve relevant documents even for short or single-term queries.

There are several exciting directions for future work. First, we plan to expand the coverage of our medical knowledge graph using more comprehensive knowledge resources. Second, we intend to explore more sophisticated entity-linking techniques beyond simple lexical matching. Third, to enable deployment on resource-constrained IoT devices, we will construct a vector database of the encoded document embeddings and load it directly onto the target hardware. This will circumvent the need for inference-time encoding and drastically reduce retrieval latency and memory overhead. Finally, we aim to implement an end-to-end prototype for real-time clinical decision support on medical IoT devices.

Acknowledgement. We would like to acknowledge the financial support provided by the Postgraduate Research Scholarship (PGRS) at Xi'an Jiaotong-Liverpool University (contract number PGRS2006013). Additionally, this research has received partial funding from the Jiangsu Science and Technology Programme (contract number BK20221260).

References

1. Alsentzer, E., et al.: Publicly available clinical Bert embeddings. arXiv preprint arXiv:1904.03323 (2019)
2. Boteva, V., Gholipour, D., Sokolov, A., Riezler, S.: A full-text learning to rank dataset for medical information retrieval. In: Ferro, N., et al. (eds.) ECIR 2016. LNCS, vol. 9626, pp. 716–722. Springer, Cham (2016). https://doi.org/10.1007/978-3-319-30671-1_58
3. Christopher, D., Raghavan, P., Schütze, H., et al.: Scoring term weighting and the vector space model. Introduction Inf. Retrieval **100**, 2–4 (2008)
4. Dai, Z., Callan, J.: Context-aware term weighting for first stage passage retrieval. In: Association for Computing Machinery, SIGIR 2020, pp. 1533–1536. New York, NY, USA (2020). https://doi.org/10.1145/3397271.3401204
5. Dai, Z., Xiong, C., Callan, J., Liu, Z.: Convolutional neural networks for soft-matching n-grams in ad-hoc search. In: Proceedings of the Eleventh ACM International Conference on Web Search and Data Mining, pp. 126–134 (2018)
6. Devlin, J., Chang, M.W., Lee, K., Toutanova, K.: BERT: pre-training of deep bidirectional transformers for language understanding. In: Proceedings of the 2019 Conference of the North American Chapter of the Association for Computational Linguistics: Human Language Technologies, Volume 1 (Long and Short Papers), pp. 4171–4186. Association for Computational Linguistics, Minneapolis, Minnesota (2019). https://doi.org/10.18653/v1/N19-1423. URL https://aclanthology.org/N19-1423

7. Dimitrov, D.V.: Medical internet of things and big data in healthcare. Healthc. Inf. Res. **22**(3), 156–163 (2016)
8. Elhoseny, M., Ramírez-González, G., Abu-Elnasr, O.M., Shawkat, S.A., Arunkumar, N., Farouk, A.: Secure medical data transmission model for IoT-based healthcare systems. IEEE Access **6**, 20596–20608 (2018)
9. Grover, A., Leskovec, J.: node2vec: scalable feature learning for networks. In: Proceedings of the 22nd ACM SIGKDD International Conference on Knowledge Discovery and Data Mining, pp. 855–864 (2016)
10. Huang, P.S., He, X., Gao, J., Deng, L., Acero, A., Heck, L.: Learning deep structured semantic models for web search using clickthrough data. In: Proceedings of the 22nd ACM International Conference on Information & Knowledge Management, pp. 2333–2338 (2013)
11. Johnson, A., Bulgarelli, L., Pollard, T., Horng, S., Celi, L.A., Mark, R.: Mimic-iv. PhysioNet (2020). https://physionet.org/content/mimiciv/1.0/. Accessed 23 Aug 2021
12. Johnson, A.E., et al.: Mimic-iii, a freely accessible critical care database. Sci. Data **3**(1), 1–9 (2016)
13. raj Kanakarajan, K., Kundumani, B., Abraham, A., Sankarasubbu, M.: BioSim-CSE: biomedical sentence embeddings using contrastive learning. In: Proceedings of the 13th International Workshop on Health Text Mining and Information Analysis (LOUHI), pp. 81–86 (2022)
14. Karpukhin, V., et al.: Dense passage retrieval for open-domain question answering. arXiv preprint arXiv:2004.04906 (2020)
15. Kim, S.W., Gil, J.M.: Research paper classification systems based on TF-IDF and LDA schemes. HCIS **9**, 1–21 (2019)
16. Li, Y., Wehbe, R.M., Ahmad, F.S., Wang, H., Luo, Y.: A comparative study of pretrained language models for long clinical text. J. Am. Med. Inform. Assoc. **30**(2), 340–347 (2023)
17. Lipscomb, C.E.: Medical subject headings (mesh). Bull. Med. Libr. Assoc. **88**(3), 265 (2000)
18. Liu, Y., et al.: RoBERTa: a robustly optimized BERT pretraining approach. arXiv preprint arXiv:1907.11692 (2019)
19. Lu, Z.X., et al.: Application of AI and IoT in clinical medicine: summary and challenges. Curr. Med. Sci. **41**, 1134–1150 (2021)
20. Nogueira, R., Yang, W., Lin, J., Cho, K.: Document expansion by query prediction. arXiv preprint arXiv:1904.08375 (2019)
21. Raffel, C., et al.: Exploring the limits of transfer learning with a unified text-to-text transformer. J. Mach. Learn. Res. **21**(1), 5485–5551 (2020)
22. Reimers, N., Gurevych, I.: Sentence-BERT: sentence embeddings using siamese BERT-networks. In: Proceedings of the 2019 Conference on Empirical Methods in Natural Language Processing and the 9th International Joint Conference on Natural Language Processing (EMNLP-IJCNLP), pp. 3982–3992 (2019)
23. Robertson, S.E., Walker, S., Jones, S., Hancock-Beaulieu, M.M., Gatford, M., et al.: Okapi at TREC-3. Nist Special Publication Sp **109**, 109 (1995)
24. Shen, Y., He, X., Gao, J., Deng, L., Mesnil, G.: Learning semantic representations using convolutional neural networks for web search. In: Proceedings of the 23rd International Conference on World Wide Web, pp. 373–374 (2014)
25. Sparck Jones, K.: A statistical interpretation of term specificity and its application in retrieval. J. Documentation **28**(1), 11–21 (1972)

26. Speer, R., Chin, J., Havasi, C.: ConceptNet 5.5: an open multilingual graph of general knowledge. In: Proceedings of the AAAI Conference on Artificial Intelligence, vol. 31 (2017)
27. Taori, R., et al.: Alpaca: a strong, replicable instruction-following model. Stanford Center Res. Found. Models **3**(6), 7 (2023). https://crfm.stanford.edu/2023/03/13/alpaca.html
28. Thakur, N., Reimers, N., Rücklé, A., Srivastava, A., Gurevych, I.: BEIR: a heterogeneous benchmark for zero-shot evaluation of information retrieval models. In: Thirty-Fifth Conference on Neural Information Processing Systems Datasets and Benchmarks Track (Round 2) (2021). https://openreview.net/forum?id=wCu6T5xFjeJ
29. Touvron, H., et al.: Llama: open and efficient foundation language models. arXiv preprint arXiv:2302.13971 (2023)
30. Wadden, D., et al.: Fact or fiction: verifying scientific claims. In: Proceedings of the 2020 Conference on Empirical Methods in Natural Language Processing (EMNLP), pp. 7534–7550 (2020)
31. Wang, W., Wei, F., Dong, L., Bao, H., Yang, N., Zhou, M.: MiniLM: deep self-attention distillation for task-agnostic compression of pre-trained transformers. Adv. Neural. Inf. Process. Syst. **33**, 5776–5788 (2020)
32. Zhang, Y., Chen, Q., Yang, Z., Lin, H., Lu, Z.: BioWordVec, improving biomedical word embeddings with subword information and MeSH. Sci. Data **6**(1), 52 (2019)

Deep Recognition of Chinese Herbal Medicines Based on a Caputo Fractional Order Convolutional Neural Network

Tao Li[1,2], Jiawei Yang[1], Chenxi Li[1], Lulu Lv[1], Kang Liu[2],
Zhipeng Yuan[2], Youyong Li[3], and Hongqing Yu[4(✉)]

[1] College of Railway Transportation, Hunan University of Technology, Zhuzhou,
China
litao@hut.edu.cn
[2] Department of Computer Science, University of Sheffield, Sheffield, UK
{kang.liu,zhipeng.yuan}@sheffield.ac.uk
[3] Hubei Provincial Hospital of Traditional Chinese Medicine, Wuhan, China
lyyzyy@yeah.net
[4] School of Computing and Engineering, University of Derby, Derby, UK
h.yu@derby.ac.uk

Abstract. Chinese herbal medicines are the treasure of Chinese traditional medicine, which contains active ingredients that have significant therapeutic effects for many diseases. To solve the fluctuation and inefficiency problems faced by the existing image recognition of Chinese herbal medicines relying on manual subjectivity, a deep classification and recognition method based on a fractional order convolutional neural network is proposed for the images of Chinese herbal medicines. This method introduces Caputo fractional order gradient descent to update the model parameters, which improves the accuracy of gradient descent in the process of training the model, and solves the problem that integer order gradient descent is prone to fall into the local optimal solution and thus leads to low accuracy. By establishing a multi-scale standard Chinese herbal medicines dataset, the feature recognition ability based on Caputo Fractional Order Convolutional Neural Network (CFO-CNN) is trained and tested. And at the same time, the fractional order backpropagation function is used, so that the model can effectively find the global optimal solution, and achieve the output of the feature deep recognition. Experiments show that the method can effectively achieve the deep classification recognition of Chinese herbal medicines varieties, species and grades.

Keywords: Fractional Order · Convolutional Neural Network · Chinese herbal medicines · Image classification

1 Introduction

As an important part of traditional Chinese medicine, the active ingredients of Chinese herbal medicines can be used in the prevention and treatment of diseases,

© The Author(s), under exclusive license to Springer Nature Switzerland AG 2024
J. Qi and P. Yang (Eds.): IoTBDH 2023, CCIS 2019, pp. 41–51, 2024.
https://doi.org/10.1007/978-3-031-52216-1_4

and it is also very important to accurately identify their traits. In traditional trait identification, Chinese herbal medicines are often classified and identified by human subjective behaviors such as tasting, sniffing, and eye observation. However, many herbs are morphologically similar but have different effects, e.g., Psyllium and Cuscuta, which makes it difficult to classify and identify herbs on a large scale using only the human appearance of the herbs.

The application of automation and intelligent technology to medical and health services is of great significance to enhance the development of medical care [1,2]. To improve the accuracy and consistency of the trait identification technology of Chinese herbal medicines, the study of how to break through the traditional trait identification methods of Chinese herbal medicines using machine learning-based image recognition and classification techniques has become a hot research issue. Article [3] proposes the use of Attention Pyramid Networks for the recognition of Chinese herbal medicines, introducing competitive attention and spatial collaborative attention applied to the recognition of Chinese herbal medicines. The authors in the article [4] utilize a mutual triple attention learning approach that allows two student networks to collaborate on parameter updates. Meng Han et al. [5] classified Chinese herbal medicines through a new mutual learning model that could extract stronger and richer features without increasing the parameter size. Although the above deep learning methods can identify the image types of some Chinese herbal medicines, they do not consider that there are different varieties of the same kind of Chinese herbal medicines, and the same variety has different specifications, quality, and price. The traditional deep learning model-based image recognition and classification methods for Chinese herbal medicines are facing significant challenges.

Convolutional neural network (CNN) is one of the main deep learning models [6,7], which has attracted much attention because of its outstanding advantages in image recognition and classification. CNN has been widely used to solve image recognition problems in many fields of production and life, such as portrait recognition [8], plant disease identification [9–11], QR code recognition [12], Human Activity Recognition [13], and so on. Meanwhile, optimizing CNN using fractional order is an important method in the field of deep learning, and some studies [14,15] have shown that the fractional order gradient method can avoid the problem of the CNN model falling into the local optimal solution. Therefore, this paper investigates a Caputo fractional order Convolutional Neural Network (CFO-CNN) based method to achieve deep recognition of Chinese herbal medicines images. The main contributions of this paper include:

1. A model structure based on CFO-CNN is proposed. This model adopts Caputo fractional order gradient descent instead of integer order gradient descent to update the model parameters. By doing so, it addresses the issue of the integer order gradient descent algorithm's susceptibility to local optima due to fine-grained defects. The optimization of the backpropagation algorithm improves the recognition accuracy of the model.
2. A convolutional neural network model incorporating the fractional order gradient descent method applied to Chinese herbal medicines is proposed. This

model can achieve deep classification recognition of multiple Chinese herbal medicines varieties, species, and grades. It solves the problem of fluctuation and inefficiency faced by manual subjective identification of Chinese herbal medicines, which is of great significance in improving the clinical application of Chinese herbal medicines.

2   Approach

In this paper, a Caputo Fractional Order Gradient Descent Convolutional Neural Network (CFO-CNN) for deep classification and recognition of Chinese herbal medicines is proposed to extract features from the data of Chinese herbal medicines using a convolutional neural network. The fractional order gradient descent method is used to update the extracted parameter information in the model and continuously optimize the parameters in the feature extraction process to improve the classification and recognition of Chinese herbal medicines.

There is no publicly available dataset in the field of Chinese herbal medicines identification and classification. In this paper, we extracted images of various Chinese herbal medicines from web pages in different scenes and different backgrounds to form a dataset, and manually created the label information for each variety of herbs. The images of different varieties, species, and grades of different herbal medicines are used as datasets and input data x to the neural network model, and the feature expressions of herbal medicines are obtained through convolutional feature extraction

$$x_j^{(l)} = f\left(\sum_{(i=1)}^{l} w_{ij}^{(l)} * x_i^{(l-1)} + b_j^{(l)} \right) \tag{1}$$

where $x_j^{(l-1)}$ denotes the Chinese herbal medicines data information of the layer i channel of layer $l - 1$, $f(\cdot)$ denotes the activation function, $w_{ij}^{(l)}$ denotes the weight of the convolutional layer l, $b_j^{(l)}$ denotes the bias term of layer l, and $x_i^{(l)}$ is the output of Chinese herbal medicines features of the j channel of convolutional layer l.

In the backpropagation, the *Loss* function Loss updates the parameters learned by the network, and the gradient is updated in the traditional integer order of

$$w_{k+1} = w_k - \mu \frac{\partial Loss}{\partial w_k} \tag{2}$$

$$b_{k+1} = b_k - \mu \frac{\partial Loss}{\partial b_k} \tag{3}$$

where w_k and b_k denote the current weights and bias information, w_{k+1} and b_{k+1} denote the updated weights and bias information. μ denotes the learning rate of the gradient descent algorithm. In non-convex function problems, the objective function may have multiple local optimal solutions and only one global optimal solution. The fine-grained defects of the integer order gradient descent algorithm lead to falling into local optimal solutions in the gradient update. To improve the model identification accuracy of gradient descent and prevent the problem of falling into local optimal solutions during updating, the Caputo fractional order derivative is introduced, and the general form of Caputo fractional order derivative is obtained after the sum of partial integrals [16] as

$$
{}_a^C D_x^\alpha f(t) = \sum_n^\infty \frac{f^{(n)}(t_0)}{\Gamma(n+1-\alpha)} (t-t_0)^{n-\alpha} \tag{4}
$$

where ${}_a^C D_x^\alpha$ is an operator of Caputo fractional order, α denotes the order, and when α is a positive integer, it denotes the integer order derivative in, the usual sense. When denoting the fractional order, it is necessary to satisfy $n-1 < \alpha < n$, where $n \in N+$ and $\Gamma(\alpha) = \int_0^\infty x^{\alpha-1} e^{-x} dx$ is the Gamma function. Each time the feature parameters are updated by Caputo fractional order gradient descent. The updated characteristic parameter information of Chinese herbal medicines that can be obtained by combining Eq. (2), Eq. (3) and Eq. (4) can be expressed as

$$
w_{k+1}^* = w_k - \mu_a^C D_x^\alpha Loss(w) \tag{5}
$$

$$
b_{k+1}^* = w_k - \mu_b^C D_x^\alpha Loss(b) \tag{6}
$$

where w_{k+1}^* and b_{k+1}^* denote the updated weights and biases of the fractional order gradient descent method, w_k and b_k denote the current weights and biases, $\mu_a^C D_x^\alpha Loss(w)$ denotes the derivatives of the Caputo fractional order concerning the current weights w, and $\mu_b^C D_x^\alpha Loss(b)$ denotes the derivative of the Caputo fractional order concerning the current bias b. After Taylor expands the Caputo fractional order and retains the results of the first term, Eq. (5) and Eq. (6) can be rewritten as follows

$$
w_{k+1}^* = w_k - \mu \frac{f^{(1)}(w_k-1)}{\Gamma(2-\alpha)} |w_k - w_{k-1}|^{(1-\alpha)} \tag{7}
$$

$$
b_{k+1}^* = b_k - \mu \frac{f^{(1)}(b_k-1)}{\Gamma(2-\alpha)} |b_k - b_{k-1}|^{(1-\alpha)} \tag{8}
$$

where w_{k-1} and b_{k-1} denote the weights and biases of the last time. After many iterations, the feature parameters of the final output image of Chinese herbal medicines are classified by Softmax function, and the probability of different varieties, species and grades under different species of Chinese herbal medicines obtained can be expressed as follows

$$
P = \begin{cases} Softmax\left(\sum_{v=1}^l w_v^{*(l)} x^{(l-1)} + b_v^{*(l)}\right), x \in x_{variaty} \\ Softmax\left(\sum_{s=1}^l w_s^{*(l)} x^{(l-1)} + b_s^{*(l)}\right), x \in x_{specias} \\ Softmax\left(\sum_{g=1}^l w_g^{*(l)} x^{(l-1)} + b_g^{*(l)}\right), x \in x_{grade} \end{cases} \tag{9}
$$

P denotes the probability of identifying different varieties, species and different grades of herbs under the same species. $x_{variety}$ denotes the variable data of herbal medicines, $x_{species}$ denotes the species data of Chinese herbal medicines, x_{grade} denotes the data of different grades of Chinese herbal medicines under the same type of herb. The deep classification and recognition method of Chinese herbal medicines based on Caputo fractional order convolutional neural network is shown in Fig. 1

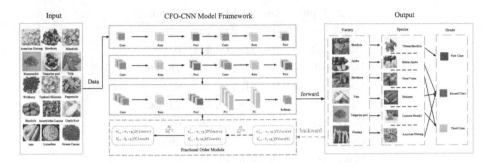

Fig. 1. Deep classification recognition system for Chinese herbal medicines based on Caputo fractional order convolutional neural network

3   Experiments

Through tests of Chinese herbal medicine picture classification and identification, the study is methodically assessed. Image recognition shows this method's benefits over previous deep learning-based categorization approaches for Chinese herbal medicines.

Chinese herbal medicine image identification is not restricted to a particular setting, one event, or even one database [17]. Here, the experiment's data consists of randomly selected photos of Chinese herbal medicines against various backdrops and scenarios from the Chinese herbal medicines dataset. The data contains nine representative Chinese herbs, each with about 700 images, and a total of about 6300 images of Chinese herbal medicines as training data and about 100 images as test data, which are annotated by manually labeling the data with labels that include the variety, species and grade of the Chinese herbal medicines. After loading the Chinese herbal medicines dataset, the data resolution is set to 224 × 224, and the step size of each experiment is 16. Convolutional pooling is used to down-sample the images of Chinese herbal medicines; the fully connected layer provides parameter information in dimensionality reduction; fractional order gradient optimization is used to optimize the parameters for backpropagation; and lastly, visualization is applied to the experimental results. The parameter settings of the CFO-CNN model used in this study are shown in Table 1.

The model uses five convolutional layers and pooling layers to downsample the input data, the first fully connected layer spreads the down-sampled feature maps into one-dimensional vectors, and the second fully connected layer outputs the dimensions of the number of varieties of herbs to be recognized for the final classification prediction of Chinese herbal medicines.

Table 1. Parameters of the CFO-CNN model

Layer (type)	Output Shape	Param #
Conv2d-1	[16, 32, 222, 222]	896
MaxPool2d-2	[16, 32, 111, 111]	0
Conv2d-3	[16, 64, 109, 109]	18,496
MaxPool2d-4	[16, 64, 54, 54]	0
Conv2d-5	[16, 128, 52, 52]	73,856
MaxPool2d-6	[16, 128, 26, 26]	0
Conv2d-7	[16, 256, 24, 24]	295,168
MaxPool2d-8	[16, 256, 12, 12]	0
Conv2d-9	[16, 256, 10, 10]	590,080
MaxPool2d-10	[16, 256, 5, 5]	0
Conv2d-11	[16, 512, 3, 3]	1,180,160
MaxPool2d-12	[16, 512, 1, 1]	0
Linear-13	[16, 128]	65,664
Linear-14	[16, 9]	1,161

From the test dataset, a random selection of Chinese herbal medicine images was used to create test data, which the CFO-CNN model then categorized. Fig. A identified this set of Chinese herbal data as Bark, Leaf, Hawthorn, Tuckahoe, Medlar, Ganoderma lucidum, Rattan, Cordyceps, and Panax notoginseng. From the figure, it can be seen that the CFO-CNN proposed in this study can classify accurately all the Chinese herbal medicines given by the test.

Three plants were identified as belonging to the Ginseng variety-Panax ginseng, Codonopsis, and Radix glehniae-after deep recognition of the Chinese herb varieties was carried out, as shown in Fig. B. Three herbs were recognized under the variety of Ginger as Dried ginger, Curcuma and Baked. Three herbs were identified under the variety of Chrysanthemum, namely Wormwood, Taraxacum, and Daisy. The CFO-CNN is very accurate for deep recognition of different species in the variety of Chinese herbal medicines as shown in Fig. B.

Fig. C demonstrated the analysis of different classes of herbs according to their respective classes, in which it was identified that in Ginseng, Panax ginseng belongs to the first class, Radix glehniae is second class, Codonopsis belongs to the third class. Ginger Curcuma is first class, Baked ginger is second class, and Dried ginger belongs to the third class. In Chrysanthemum Daisy is first class, Wormwood is second class, and Taraxacum belongs to third class. From Fig. A, Fig. B, and Fig. C, it can be judged that the convolutional neural network based on fractional order gradient descent can deeply classify and identify the classes of Chinese herbs, different kinds of herbs under different herb classes as well as different grades of the same kind of herbs, and the results are accurate.

Compare the effect of fractional order gradient descent CNN algorithm and integer order gradient descent algorithm in the task of Chinese herbal medicines classification and recognition. Fig. D compares ResNet18, GoogLeNet, MobileNet with CFO-CNN. Because of the fractional order compared to the integer order's complex computational form, under the same Chinese herbal medicines dataset, the convolutional neural network with fractional order gradient descent method is about 7.5% more accurate than the traditional ResNet18 model, about 4% more accurate than the traditional GoogLeNet model, and about 23% more accurate compared to the traditional MobileNet model, which is a significant improvement in the accuracy.

The varying convergence speeds exhibited by fractional orders greater than one and less than one. To further compare different orders of gradient descent algorithms, Fig. E selected and compared the accuracy of model recognition for traditional Chinese medicine at different orders. The resulting accuracy change curve graph reveals insights. Analyzing the range of fractional orders, it's evident that for fractional orders of 0.1, 0.4, and 0.7, when the fractional order is less than one, the performance of fractional order gradient descent algorithms is inferior to both integer order gradient descent algorithms and fractional order gradient descent algorithms greater than one. When the order is greater than one, as seen from the curves at fractional orders of 1.3 and 1.7, fractional order gradient descent algorithms show significant improvement compared to first-order integer order algorithms. Analyzing the magnitude of fractional orders, it's evident from the curves at orders 0.1, 1.9, and 1.3 that the further the order is from the corresponding integer order, the worse the gradient descent performance becomes. Conversely, when the order is greater and closer to the corresponding integer order, the advantages of fractional order gradient descent algorithms become prominent. To illustrate, a point-line graph was created based on the maximum accuracy values for different orders after 150 iterations. In the case of integer order gradient descent algorithms, the obtained accuracy was 87%. When the fractional order is 1.3, the accuracy of the fractional order gradient descent algorithm reaches 95.5%, reflecting an enhancement of 8.5% compared to integer orders. Conversely, when the fractional order is 0.1, the fractional order contributes almost negligibly to parameter updates.

Fig. F compares the gradient descent method with fractional orders of 0.7, 1.0 and 1.3. It is obvious from the figure that when the order is 1.3, the function has converged to the extremum point after about 120 iterations, and the loss error is about 0.12. When the order is 1.0, the function has completed convergence in 60 iterations, but the error is larger, about 0.88, which is not satisfactory. The convergence is not satisfactory. When the order is 0.7, the model stops converging after 90 iterations with an error of about 1.04, and the model performs poorly in recognizing Chinese herbal medicines during training. It can be seen that when the order of the fractional order is larger than the integer order and the closer to the integer order, the better the convergence of the gradient descent method of fractional order is, on the contrary, when the order is far away from the integer order or smaller than the integer order, the model is easy to fall into the local optimal solution. From this, it can be determined that the value of the order of the fractional order gradient descent method should be elected as 1.3 in the deep classification and recognition task of Chinese herbal medicines.

In Fig. G, the CFO-CNN learning recognition accuracy by fractional order gradient descent method is compared with various network models' deep learning techniques. For the comparative experiment, the deep learning models Resnet18, GoogLeNet, and MobileNet are chosen. The box plot indicates that when compared to the conventional deep learning Chinese herbal medicine image recognition method, the accuracy of the convolutional neural network with the Caputo fractional order gradient descent method is improved by at least 4%. Additionally, the results of multiple experiments are stable and reliable. The reason for this is that the traditional artificial neural network for the image recognition of Chinese herbal medicines is based on the computational rules of integer order gradient descent to update the weight information, while this paper adopts the fractional order gradient descent method to introduce Caputo fractional order to update the weights, which is superior to the non-local nature of the fractional order that allows it to better capture the global information, and its update method is more accurate compared to that of the integer order updating method.

Fig. H compares the loss values of the models derived from the loss function based on the learning process of Chinese herbal medicine photos in order to further compare the gradient descent techniques at various orders. We find that the ultimate loss value of the model decreases minimally as the fractional order moves farther away from the integer order, suggesting that gradient updates are not clearly affected by this change. The computed loss values from the loss function computation are reduced when the fractional order approaches an integer order and exceeds the first-order integer. This suggests that picture learning recognition gets more accurate, which is better for correctly identifying and categorizing Chinese herbal medicines.

The confusion matrix used in this study to identify nine Chinese herbal types is displayed in Fig. 2. The information reveals that the estimated probability of identifying Panax ginseng is approximately 100%, that of identifying Codonopsis is 100%, that of identifying Radix glehniae is 95.6%, that of identifying Dried ginger is 99.8%, that of Baking ginger is 87.9%, that of Curcuma is 87.3%, that of Wormwood is 100%, that of Daisy with 84.4% predicted probability, and that of Taraxacum with 88% predicted probability. It can be seen that the convolutional neural network based on the fractional order gradient descent method has high accuracy in predicting multi-class Chinese herbal medicines varieties, and the recognition accuracy of similar different kinds of Chinese herbal medicines can reach more than 80% even under the same class.

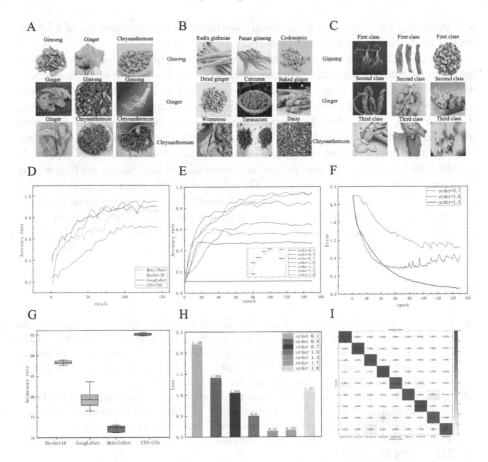

Fig. 2. A represents the class of herbs recognized by the model; B is the corresponding variety of the recognized herbs; C is the classification of the recognized herb classes; D is the experimental comparison plot of integer order gradient descent and fractional order gradient descent convolutional neural networks with different models; E represents the recognition ability of fractional order gradient descent with different orders; F is a plot of the error analysis for different orders of the fractional order; G is the boxplot of the recognition effect of different models; H is the magnitude of the loss value of Chinese herbs at different orders; I is the confusion matrix of a certain nine varieties of herbs.

4   Conclusion

In this paper, a fractional order convolutional neural network based on gradient descent is investigated for deep recognition and classification of Chinese herbal medicine images. Among them, the model adopts Caputo fractional order gradient descent instead of integer order gradient descent method to update the CNN model parameters, solve the problem that the simple computation rule of integer order leads to easily fall into the local optimal solution, optimizing the network backpropagation algorithm. Improved model convergence performance and improved the accuracy of the deep classification and recognition of Chinese herbal medicines images by about 8.5%.

This CFO-CNN model can realize the variety recognition of different Chinese herbal medicines, further identify the species of Chinese herbal medicines under different varieties of Chinese herbal medicines, and distinguish different grades under the same type of Chinese herbal medicines according to the advantages and disadvantages, which solves the fluctuation in the classification of Chinese herbal medicines due to manual subjectivity and the inefficiency of manual recognition.

The main limitation of this paper is that its data sources are only randomly grabbed from several Chinese herbal medicine image databases, and thus may not cover all types of Chinese herbs. Therefore, datasets covering more types of Chinese herbs are needed to improve the breadth and persuasiveness, and further research and experiments are needed to fully evaluate the performance and feasibility of the present method for the application of Chinese herbal medicines recognition.

References

1. Deng, Z., Yang, P., Zhao, Y., Zhao, X., Dong, F.: Life-logging data aggregation solution for interdisciplinary healthcare research and collaboration. In: 2015 IEEE International Conference on Computer and Information Technology; Ubiquitous Computing and Communications; Dependable, Autonomic and Secure Computing; Pervasive Intelligence and Computing, pp. 2315–2320 (2015)
2. Spanakis, E.G., et al.: Myhealthavatar: personalized and empowerment health services through internet of things technologies. In: 2014 4th International Conference on Wireless Mobile Communication and Healthcare-Transforming Healthcare Through Innovations in Mobile and Wireless Technologies (MOBIHEALTH), pp. 331–334. IEEE (2014)
3. Xu, Y., et al.: Multiple attentional pyramid networks for Chinese herbal recognition. Pattern Recogn. **110**, 107558 (2021)
4. Hao, W., Han, M., Li, S., Li, F., et al.: MTAL: a novel Chinese herbal medicine classification approach with mutual triplet attention learning. Wirel. Commun. Mob. Comput. **2022**, 9 (2022)
5. Han, M., Zhang, J., Zeng, Y., Hao, F., Ren, Y.: A novel method of Chinese herbal medicine classification based on mutual learning. Mathematics **10**(9), 1557 (2022)
6. Yao, G., Lei, T., Zhong, J.: A review of convolutional-neural-network-based action recognition. Pattern Recogn. Lett. **118**, 14–22 (2019)
7. Dhillon, A., Verma, G.K.: Convolutional neural network: a review of models, methodologies and applications to object detection. Prog. Artif. Intell. **9**(2), 85–112 (2020)
8. Lou, G., Shi, H.: Face image recognition based on convolutional neural network. China Commun. **17**(2), 117–124 (2020)
9. Liu, B., Zhang, Y., He, D., Li, Y.: Identification of apple leaf diseases based on deep convolutional neural networks. Symmetry **10**(1), 11 (2017)
10. Bhujel, A., Kim, N., Arulmozhi, E., Basak, J., Kim, H.: A lightweight attention-based convolutional neural networks for tomato leaf disease classification. Agriculture 2022 **12**, 228 (2022)

11. Lu, Y., Yi, S., Zeng, N., Liu, Y., Zhang, Y.: Identification of rice diseases using deep convolutional neural networks. Neurocomputing **267**, 378–384 (2017)
12. Wang, J., Qin, J., Xiang, X., Tan, Y., Pan, N.: College of computer science and information technology, central south university of forestry and technology, 498 shaoshan s rd, Changsha, 410004, China, "captcha recognition based on deep convolutional neural network,". Math. Biosci. Eng. **16**(5), 5851–5861 (2019)
13. Yang, P., Yang, C., Lanfranchi, V., Ciravegna, F.: Activity graph based convolutional neural network for human activity recognition using acceleration and gyroscope data. IEEE Trans. Industr. Inf. **18**(10), 6619–6630 (2022)
14. Wang, Y., He, Y., Zhu, Z.: Study on fast speed fractional order gradient descent method and its application in neural networks. Neurocomputing **489**, 366–376 (2022)
15. Sheng, D., Wei, Y., Chen, Y., Wang, Y.: Convolutional neural networks with fractional order gradient method. Neurocomputing **408**, 42–50 (2020)
16. Podlubny, I., Chechkin, A., Skovranek, T., Chen, Y., Jara, B.M.V.: Matrix approach to discrete fractional calculus ii: partial fractional differential equations. J. Comput. Phys. **228**(8), 3137–3153 (2009)
17. Sun, X., Qian, H.: Chinese herbal medicine image recognition and retrieval by convolutional neural network. PLoS ONE **11**(6), e0156327 (2016)

Randomized Multi-task Feature Learning Approach for Modelling and Predicting Alzheimer's Disease Progression

Xulong Wang[1], Yu Zhang[1], Menghui Zhou[1], Tong Liu[1], Zhipeng Yuan[1], Xiyang Peng[1], Kang Liu[1], Jun Qi[2], and Po Yang[1($\boxtimes$)]

[1] Department of Computer Science, University of Sheffield, Sheffield, UK
{xl.wang,yzhang489,mzhou47,zhipeng.yuan,xpeng24,
kang.liu,po.yang}@sheffield.ac.uk
[2] Department of Computing, Xi'an JiaoTong-Liverpool University, Suzhou, China
Jun.Qi@xjtlu.edu.cn

Abstract. Multi-task feature learning (MTFL) methods play a key role in predicting Alzheimer's disease (AD) progression. These studies adhere to a unified feature-sharing framework to promote information exchange on relevant disease progression tasks. MTFL not only utilise the inherent properties of tasks to enhance prediction performance, but also yields weights that are capable to indicate nuanced changes of related AD biomarkers. Task regularized priors, however, introduced by MTFL lead to uncertainty in biomarkers selection, particularly amidst a plethora of highly interrelated biomarkers in a high dimensional space. There is little attention on studying how to design feasible experimental protocols for assessment of MTFL models. To narrow this knowledge gap, we proposed a **R**andomize **M**ulti-task **F**eature **L**earning (RMFL) approach to effectively model and predict AD progression. As task increases, the results show that the RMFL is not only stable and interpretable, but also reduced by 0.2 in normalized mean square error compared to single-task models like Lasso, Ridge. Our method is also adaptable as a general regression framework to predict other chronic disease progression.

Keywords: Multi-task feature learning · Alzheimer's disease · Randomization · Stability selection

1 Introduction

Alzheimer's disease, as one of the most common forms of dementia, is a neurodegenerative disease that causes problems with progressive cognitive decline and memory loss [8]. With rates projected to increase by 75% in the next quarter of a century [1], AD is a leading contributor to disability amongst older people and causes significant morbidity as well as personal family burden. So far, there is no effective cure for AD where science has not yet identified any treatments that can slow or halt the progression of this disease. Yet, early intervention and timely diagnosis could be still promising and cost-effective. It poses an important

J. Qi and P. Yang (Eds.): IoTBDH 2023, CCIS 2019, pp. 52–68, 2024.
https://doi.org/10.1007/978-3-031-52216-1_5

research area that understands how the AD progresses and identify their related pathological biomarkers for the progression. To accelerate AD's research, the Alzheimer's Disease Neuroimaging Initiative (ADNI) funded by NHI provided a large boundary of publicly available neuroimaging data including magnetic resonance imaging (MRI), positron emission tomography (PET), other biomarkers and cognitive measures for scientific study. A variety of medical data driven based machine learning techniques [9, 10, 21–23], like deep learning models [5, 11], multi-task feature learning (MTFL) model [12, 24, 26] and survival model [15, 19, 20], have been investigated to deal with these data for better prediction of AD progression. The motivation of those study is to learn a stable set of features across all tasks and share them to improve the accuracy of all tasks. However,before they share feature information, picking out stable and unbiased features is a key challenge.

Randomization as a method of machine learning has been extensively used in theoretical algorithms and real-world applications [18]. It prevents the selection bias and insures against the accidental bias. For example, in ensemble learning approaches, the Random Forest and the Extra-Trees algorithm [13, 16] belong to two averaging algorithms based on randomized decision trees. Both algorithms are perturb-and combine techniques [2] specifically designed for trees. This means a diverse set of models is created by introducing randomness in the model's construction. The prediction of the ensemble is given as the averaged prediction of the individual models. Despite the algorithms in ensemble learning have good predictive accuracy, they are black box methods which are unable to explain the reasons behind the result. Particularly in the field of medically assisted diagnosis as well as in finance, the value of model interpretability is much higher than the accuracy of its predictions.

In this paper, we introduce a randomize multi-task feature learning (RMFL) approach for effectively modelling and predicting AD progression. We examine typical MTFL models via randomized structural regularization approaches in AD study and choose two typical single task models: Ridge regression and Lasso regression. Considering that MTFL features shared parameters and representations, we further explore four potential key points affecting evaluation process of RMFL in AD study: 1) evaluation indicators: validating the model's robustness on different type of square error or correlation coefficient; 2) repeated experimental times (e.g., results of 10 repeated experiments and 100 repeated experiments are different results; 3) size and portion of training data; 4) number of tasks in MTFL (e.g., time points in AD progression). For each point, we design and set up experimental protocols for comparison and exploration, highlighting following multi-fold contributions:

- We introduce a RMFL strategy that is capable of predicting AD progression with high accuracy, while elucidating the structure that can structural nuances indicative of significant biomarkers alterations in AD.
- We provide a solid evidence that whether RMFL model perform well in complex practical experimental settings. One key finding is that MTEN's superior performance may stem from the stability selection of features across multiple

tasks. This provides a checkpoint for whether the model works well in more complex practical applications.

– By leveraging methodical validation, we demonstrate that some limitations of MTFL models in AD study: 1) the normalized mean square error emerges as the most reliable performance metric, while alternative evaluative indicators lack comparable objectivity. 2) MTEN has a considerable potential for further improvement at late stage prediction of AD progression. 3) The assumption of temporal smoothness in MTFL models for AD study constrains early task performance.

2   Methodology

2.1   Subjects

To track the effectiveness of disease progression models, ADNI-1 subjects with all corresponding MRI and cognitive scales are evaluated. The ADNI is a longitudinal multicenter study designed to develop clinical, imaging, genetic, and biochemical biomarkers for the early detection and tracking of AD. Since its launch more than a decade ago, the landmark public-private partnership has made major contributions to AD research, enabling the sharing of data between researchers around the world. A total of 800 subjects, approximately 200 normal individuals (NL), 400 subjects with Mild cognitive impairment (MCI) and 200 subjects with early AD, were involved in this study. All participants received standard clinical tests of cognitive function to be followed for 3 years, such as Mini Mental State Exam score (MMSE), Alzheimer's Disease Assessment Scale cognitive total score (ADAS-cog) and Rey Auditory Verbal Learning Test (RAVLT). The date of the participant's first visit to the hospital for screening was set as the baseline period in order to facilitate comparison with subsequent changes in the participant's status. The follow-up points, such as 6 or 12 months after the baseline point, supported the longitudinal disease progression of the subjects. For example, "M12" was defined as the follow-up survey at month 12 after baseline. As the timeline lengthens, the number of subjects who still have follow-up records gradually decreases, but detailed data at the screening stage is useful for early detection of a patient's potential risk of AD.

2.2   Image Pre-processing

For guarantee high image quality and reliable data handling, the MR images used in the paper were derived from standardized datasets, which provide the intensity normalized and gradient un-warped TI image volumes. Subsequently, the FreeSurfer image analysis suite [4] was performed to feature extraction of the MR, which executes cortical reconstruction and volumetric segmentations for processing and analyzing brain MR images. For each MRI, cortical regions and subcortical regions are generated after this pre-processing suite. For each cortical region, the cortical thickness average, standard deviation of thickness, surface area, and cortical volume were calculated as features. For each subcortical region, subcortical volume was calculated as feature. Data cleaning operations are performed:

- Removal of individuals who failed cortical reconstruction and failed quality control;
- Removal of features with more than half of the missing values;
- Individual subjects whose removal of baseline did not screen for MRI;
- Using the average of the features to fill in missing data;
- Removal of cognitive function tests in individuals with missing follow-up points in longitudinal studies.

After the pre-processing procedure, there are a total of 429 subjects and 327 MRI features.

2.3 Regression Model via Structural Regularization

Regression model has been widely used in statistical, medical and industrial applications. It is a mathematical and statistical analysis of dependent influences (independent variables) and predictors (dependent variables). Its strength lies in its strong interpretation. By fitting the data, the parameter values corresponding to the independent variable indicate its effect on the dependent variable.

We consider the problem of prediction as a linear model. In order to obtain models with generalizability, loss functions with empirical structural loss risk minimization as the formula:

$$\min_{\beta} L(y, X, \beta) + \lambda R(\beta) \tag{1}$$

where the loss term $L(y, X, \beta)$ measures how well the model fits the data, the regularization term $R(\beta)$ measures model complexity. When $\lambda \geq 0$ denotes the penalty parameters, i.e., balancing the goal of fitting the training with the goal of keeping the parameter values small, come to keep the hypothesis relatively simple in form and avoid overfitting.

In general, the sample contains a large number of possible biomarkers for the patient, such as MRI statistical values for the regional cortex, CSF, biochemical indicators and cognitive scores. They are transformed into features that can be run by the model so that the relatively important subset of features can be filtered out in the subsequent training process.

The regularization term is considered as the addition of a prior, and common paradigms are Ridge regression and Lasso, which respectively add the L_1 and L_2 norm. Statistical theory can prove that Ridge regression specifies a prior that the model obeys a Gaussian distribution and Lasso specifies a prior that the model obeys a Laplace distribution. This regularization term can be expressed as:

$$\min_{w} L(Y, X, W) + \lambda ||W||_1 \tag{2}$$

$$\min_{w} L(Y, X, W) + \lambda ||W||_2 \tag{3}$$

where ridge regression constrains variables to a smaller range for reducing some factors with little impacts on model's prediction. Unfortunately, this reduction means that these variables are still considered. To solve this problem, Lasso was proposed as a new sparse representation linear algorithm, which simultaneously performs feature selection and regression. Some variables are set to zero directly to achieve sparsity and dimensionality reduction. In addition, some randomization-based sparse algorithms [17] put in different prior assumptions to achieve the desired effect and kernel extended strategy [3] to cope with nonlinear system in complex space.

2.4   Multi-task Feature Learning

A popular setting of multi-task feature is to treat a regression model as a task. The purpose of multi-task feature learning [6] is to learn a common set of features across all tasks and share them to improve the accuracy of all tasks. Among these learning tasks, a basic assumption of MTFL is that one or more subsets are related to each other.

Let $X = [x_1, ..., x_n]^T \in \mathbb{R}^{n \times d}$ be the data matrix, $Y = [y_1, ..., y_n]^T \in \mathbb{R}^{n \times k}$ be the predicted matrix, and $W = [w_1, ..., w_k]^T \in \mathbb{R}^{d \times k}$ be the weight matrix. The process of establishing a MTL model is to estimate the value of W, which is the parameter to be estimated from the training samples.

Two common MTFL models are presented to display their properties. Multi-Task lasso is a linear model that estimates sparse coefficients for multiple regression problems jointly. The constraint is that the selected features are the same for all the regression problems, also called tasks. The Fig. 4 compares the location of the non-zero entries in the coefficient matrix W obtained with a simple Lasso or a Multi-task Lasso. Mathematically, it consists of a linear model trained with a L_{21}-norm for regularization. The objective function to minimize is:

$$\min_w \frac{1}{2n}||XW - Y||_F^2 + \alpha||W||_{21} \tag{4}$$

where $|| \cdot ||_F$ denotes the Frobenius norm $||A||_F = \sqrt{\sum_{i=1}^m \sum_{j=1}^n |a_{ij}|^2}$, and $||W||_{21}$ denotes $||W||_{21} = \sum_{i=1}^d \sqrt{\sum_{j=1}^t W_{i,j}^2}$. The multi-task lasso allows to fit multiple regression problems jointly enforcing the selected features to be the same across tasks. For example, AD cognitive progress sequential measurements, each task is a time instant, and the relevant features vary in amplitude over time while being the same. This makes feature selection by the Lasso more stable. However, when there are correlations between multiple features, the features will be randomly selected, especially when the brain region is regarded as a feature, there are some blocks with high correlation, such as atrophy of the cerebral cortex causes reduction in cortical volume and cortical thickness.

Another approach of MTFL is multi-task elastic net (MTEN). It can compensate for the shortcomings generated by multi-task lasso. When multiple features are correlated with one another, MTEN tends to select both features rather than a random. Mathematically, it consists of a linear model trained with a mixed L_{21}-norm and L_{21}-norm for regularization. The objective function to minimize is:

$$\min_{w} \frac{1}{2n}||XW - Y||_F^2 + \alpha\rho||W||_{21} + \frac{\alpha(1 - \rho)}{2}||W||_F^2 \qquad (5)$$

The difference from multi-task lasso is that MTEN adds a constraint on the F-norm of W. α and ρ controls the strictness of model penalties to trading-off the advantages between Lasso and Ridge. When $\rho = 0$, MTEN degrades to multi-task lasso; When $\alpha = 0$, MTEN degrades to traditional linear regression problem.

2.5   Randomize Multi-task Feature Learning

Randomization as a method of machine learning has been extensively used in theoretical algorithms and real-world applications [18]. It prevents the selection bias and insures against the accidental bias. For example, in embedded feature selection schemes, randomization has recently received increasing attention due to the use of randomization-related techniques to select a more stable and less biased feature subsets. Stability selection are one of them.

Stability selection is based on subsampling in combination with (high dimensional) selection algorithms. In previous related studies [24], the stability ranking score gives the probability that it is naturally interpretable. This study propose to extend a strategy of stability selection to multi-task feature study to quantify the importance of the features selected by the MTFL formulations for predicting disease progression. Multi-Task elastic network algorithm was utilized to track the area of the cerebral cortex associated with AD progression.

Let F be the overall set of features and let $f \in F$ be the subset of features by sub-sampling. Let γ denote the iteration number of sub-sampling and $Di = \{X(i), Y(i)\}$ denote one random sub-sample operation of number $i \in (0, \gamma]$. Each operation size account for $\lfloor\frac{n}{2}\rfloor$. Let Λ be the regularization parameter space. For a $\lambda \in \Lambda$, let $\hat{W}^{(i)}$ denote the model coefficient of MTFL that fitted on a subset of $D(i)$. Then, the subset of features generated in task j by the sparse constraints of the MTFL algorithm can be denote as:

$$S_j^{\lambda}(D_{(i)}) = \left\{f : \hat{W}_j^{(i)} \neq 0\right\}. \qquad (6)$$

With stability selection, we do not simply select one model in the parameter space λ. Instead the data are perturbed (e.g. by sub-sampling) γ times at task j and we choose all structures or variables that occur in a large fraction of the resulting selection sets:

$$\hat{\pi}_j^{\lambda} = \frac{\sum_{i=1}^{\gamma} I\left(f \in S_j^{\lambda}(D_{ij})\right)}{\gamma}. \qquad (7)$$

where indicator function $I(\bullet)$ denote $I(x) = \begin{cases} 1, & x = 0 \\ 0, & others \end{cases}$ and $\hat{\pi}_j^{\lambda} \in [0, 1]$ denote the stability probability of task j at MTFL approaches which feature selection is not based on individual operations but on multiple task collaboration constraints.

Repeat the above procedure for all $\lambda \in \Lambda$, we obtain the stability score $S_j(f)$ for each feature f at task j:

$$S_j(f) = \max_{\lambda \in \Lambda} \left(\hat{\pi}_j^\lambda\right). \tag{8}$$

Finally, for a cut-off π_{th} with $0 < \pi_{th} < 1$ and a set of regularization parameters Λ, the set of stable variables is defined as:

$$\hat{S}^{\text{stable}} = \{k : S_j(f) \geq \pi_{th}\} = \left\{k : \max_{\lambda \in \Lambda} \left(\hat{\pi}_j^\lambda\right) \geq \pi_{th}\right\}. \tag{9}$$

The embedded multi-task approach ensures that the selected features have the following properties:1) Stability. A cortical region of the brain that is closely related to the subject's disease progression. 2) Global significance. MTFL makes sure that the selected features are important for each task. One technique that arises here is to pick the coefficient value for one of the tasks when doing statistics on the stability of the selected features at Eq. 4. Overall, the complete stability selection procedure is shown below:

- Randomized selection of feature subsets;
- Randomly selected data subsets;
- Given a hyperparameter search range and a selected set;
- Training Multi-task model and Obtaining weighting factors;
- Polling statistics to find out the probability of a feature being selected;
- Chosen the maximum value as its final stability probability in each randomization algorithm;
- Feature selection based on a given threshold.

3   Experiment

3.1   Experiment Setup

First, experiments demonstrated that MTFL is superior in following AD progression. Combined with randomization techniques, RMFL is enable to locate the stable and sensitive cortical biomarkers. Our empirical protocol design is based on a pipeline shown in Fig. A5. The total experimental process mainly includes 5 steps: 1) split the data set; 2) select the hyper-parameters; 3) train the model; 4) evaluate the model using the test set; 5) iterate the above operations and 6) randomize multi-task feature selection strategy. Different colors denote the source or generation of different data, arrows indicate the flow of data, and serial numbers indicate the steps of the experiment.

Then, to demonstrate that the MTFL algorithm is more generalizable and stable in a variety of realistic scenarios, Four protocol is set up to explore the potential influence that the error arising from the experimental process itself: 1) evaluation indicators, 2) repeated experimental times; 3) size and portion of training data; 4) number of tasks in MTFL. In addition, the significance of randomize multi-task feature selection strategy in guiding the search for stable biomarkers was demonstrated in Experiment II visually stability biomarkers.

The evaluation metric of cross-validation is employed to evaluate the performance of AD progression model. When a metric is set in the cross-validation experiment process, a set of hyper-parameters can be obtained. By comparing the pros and cons of the results, the suitable metric for the model is finally determined. The regression performance metric often employed in MTL is normalized mean square error (nMSE) and root mean square error (rMSE) is employed to measure the performance of each specific regression task. In particular, nMSE has been normalized to each task before evaluation, so it is widely used in MTL methods based on regression tasks. Also, weighted correlation coefficient (wR) as employed in the medical literature addressing AD progression problems [7,14,25]. nMSE, rMSE and wR are defined as follows:

$$\text{nMSE}(Y, \hat{Y}) = \frac{\sum_{i=1}^{t} \left\| Y_i -, \hat{Y}_i \right\|_2^2 / \sigma(Y_i)}{\sum_{i=1}^{t} n_i} \tag{10}$$

$$\text{rMSE}(y, \hat{y}) = \sqrt{\frac{\|y - \hat{y}\|_2^2}{n}} \tag{11}$$

$$\text{wR}(Y, \hat{Y}) = \frac{\sum_{i=1}^{t} \text{Corr}\left(Y_i, \hat{Y}_i\right) n_i}{\sum_{i=1}^{t} n_i} \tag{12}$$

3.2 Experiment I Prediction with Cerebral Cortex Features

In many real-world AD application scenarios, clinicians expect the prediction model to be simple and with less input data required for giving timely early screening. In this case, it is hard to acquire both precise MRI and cognitive measures. Normally, clinicians have to spend few hours to measure AD patients' cognitive scores though some tests. Thus, one key application was considered with only MRI data as input data to predict cognitive scores at baseline and future time points. It is necessary for clinicians to perform a cognitive scale assessment, but time-consuming to complete a set of cognitive measures.

The first goal is to show a quantitative analysis of typical MTFL methods (MTEN) in comparing to single task methods (Ridge, Lasso). The external experiment setting remained consistent, with same split ratio of sample data, iteration times and features. Specifically, dataset was randomly split into training and testing sets using a ratio 9:1, i.e., models were built on 90% of the data and evaluated on the remaining 10% of the data. Models parameters were selected by 5-fold cross validation.

The results in Table 1 implies that three selected structural regularization methods are all robust (low variance). Also, MTEN models outperforms single-task learning model (Ridge and Lasso), in terms of prediction accuracy.

Table 1. Validation of AD disease progression based MTFL

	Ridge	Lasso	MTEN
Target: MMSE			
nMSE	2.088 ± 0.359	0.945 ± 0.247	**0.745 ± 0.172**
wR	0.310 ± 0.070	0.499 ± 0.034	**0.568 ± 0.053**
BL rMSE	2.841 ± 0.298	2.042 ± 0.496	**1.721 ± 0.225**
M06 rMSE	3.767 ± 0.408	2.491 ± 0.480	**2.197 ± 0.244**
M12 rMSE	3.958 ± 0.456	2.717 ± 0.587	**2.368 ± 0.535**
M24 rMSE	4.633 ± 0.579	3.320 ± 0.713	**2.944 ± 0.437**
M36 rMSE	5.745 ± 0.708	3.947 ± 0.791	**3.820 ± 0.736**
Target: ADAS-cog			
nMSE	1.147 ± 0.111	0.729 ± 0.060	**0.698 ± 0.063**
wR	0.468 ± 0.046	0.542 ± 0.052	**0.573 ± 0.044**
BL rMSE	5.465 ± 0.599	4.229 ± 0.534	**4.117 ± 0.558**
M06 rMSE	5.900 ± 0.840	4.590 ± 0.672	**4.489 ± 0.675**
M12 rMSE	6.074 ± 0.894	4.998 ± 0.754	**4.759 ± 0.620**
M24 rMSE	7.483 ± 1.200	5.818 ± 1.066	**5.761 ± 1.012**
M36 rMSE	8.905 ± 1.361	7.981 ± 1.420	**7.730 ± 1.221**

Key: MMSE, Mini-Mental State Examination; ADAS-cog, Alzheimer's Disease Assessment Scale Cognitive Subscale; BL Baseline visiting point; All algorithms were repeat 100 times and their means ± variance was counted. Represents that the result in bold is statistically significantly better than other comparison methods.

3.3   Experiment II Visually Stability Biomarkers

Experiment screened all MRI features using stability selection strategy and obtained 126 stable features, which were stable scores ≥ 0.96. Then, this feature set was put back into the MTEN algorithm to obtain a 35 stable sub-features, which can be used to track cortical biomarkers associated with AD progression. The stability vectors of stable MRI features for MMSE are shown in Fig. 1. Experiment finds that the imaging biomarkers identified by RMFL yielded promising patterns that are expected from prior knowledge on neuroimaging and cognition. Some important features are selected, such as Inferior Parietal, Hippocampus, Middle Temporal Gyri and Fusiform, are relevant to the cognitive function.

3.4   Experiment III Evaluation Indicators

In MTFL for AD study, cross-validation with evaluation metric is widely utilised to select suitable model hyper-parameters. Fair hyper-parameters could make MTFL models have better generalization performance. When an evaluation indicator is set in cross-validation experiment process, a set of hyper-parameters can

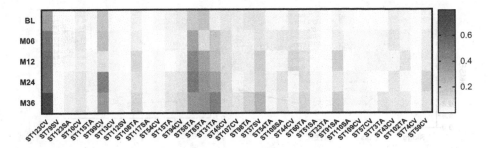

Fig. 1. Thermogram of MRI stability features by multi-task elastic net. Each column represents a cortical region of the brain selected by randomization technique.

be obtained. By comparing the pros and cons of the results, the suitable metric for the model is finally determined. However, different metrics have different preferences and emphasis on the model. It has become a consensus to employ metrics to evaluate the pros and cons of models.

Three models (Lasso, TGL and MTEN) are selected for evaluation. Dataset was randomly split into training and testing sets using a ratio 9:1. Models parameters were selected by 5-fold cross validation. The mean and standard deviation based on 20 iterations of experiments. The experimental results in Table 2 showed that selection of evaluation metrics significantly affect performance assessment of MTFL models.

According to our results, therefore, it can be seen that 1) the results obtained by metrics such as square error (MSE, rMSE, nMSE) are basically the same; 2) nMSE is the best indicator to evaluate these models due to relatively stable performance. The reason is that data distribution of each task is not the same, sharing with each other will have the effect of noise. Therefore, using the variance of tasks in nMSE will reduce the impact of task differences, and the results can better take into account each other's tasks.

3.5   Experiment IV Repeated Experimental Times

In MTFL for AD study, one typical consensus is that one experiment result is usually accidental and unreliable. To reduce experiment accidental errors, repeated experiments are required. Therefore, we evaluate the performance of four MTFL models under different repeated experimental times. We conducted 6 sets of experiments, and the number of iterations in each set was 5, 10, 20, 30, 40, 50, 100. Also, in each set of experiments, other conditions remained the same. The final result is shown in Fig. 6. The horizontal axis represents iteration, the vertical axis represents the nMSE value of each algorithm, and different colors represent algorithm. In Fig. 6, it appears that the effect of different experiments on three algorithms are visually observed. MTEN models maintains good performance in each set of experiments. From the fluctuation range of the model mean: Ridge not only performs poorly overall, but also has a large range of

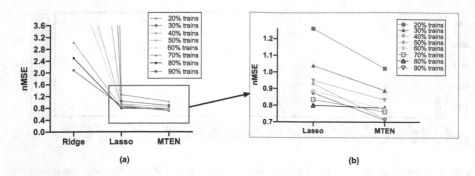

Fig. 2. nMSE values for predicting MMSE cognitive scores under different data size. Each colour label indicates the proportion of the training set in the overall.

fluctuations, which may be the reason for the under-fitting. As the number of iterations increased, three algorithms are fluctuating to varying degrees. Lasso and MTNE are relatively less affected, which implies that sparsity plays a key role in real-world scenarios.

3.6 Experiment V Size and Portion of Training Data

One significant advantage of MTFL is to deal with the issue of missing data and reduce the risk of overfitting. To prove this assumption, we evaluate different portion of training AD data over these MTFL models. Experiment train four MTL models with datasets of different data sizes with 8 groups of experiment performances. Data was split into training and test sets according to the ratio (2: 8, 3: 7, 4: 6, 5: 5, 6: 4, 7: 3, 8: 2, and 9: 1) respectively. For example, in order to compare the experimental results, the other condition settings of each group of experiments are kept consistent: datasets with MMSE scores as learning labels are conducted, with 429 and 425 samples respectively. The same data set was used to predict the trend of cognitive scores of the MMSE and ADAS-cog scales at baseline and in the next three years. The result based on 50 iterations of experiments on different splits of data using 5-fold cross validation. Each group of experiments uses 3 algorithms (Ridge, Lasso, and MTEN) for comparison. The results are shown in the Fig. 2 (a). The finding shows that: Ridge and Lasso have high overfitting risks but MTEN show advantages. In addition, to clarify the difference in performance between Lasso and MTEN, Fig. 2 (b) is the comparison of Lasso and MTEN in detail, connecting the mean two points with a straight line whose slope is less than zero, implying that MTEN is optimal for global training processes.

3.7 Experiment VI Number of Tasks in MTFL

Final key issue to MTFL models is to explore the sharing knowledge between multiple tasks. The common method is to propose an assumption and then transform into a constraint and put into an optimization function. But whether this

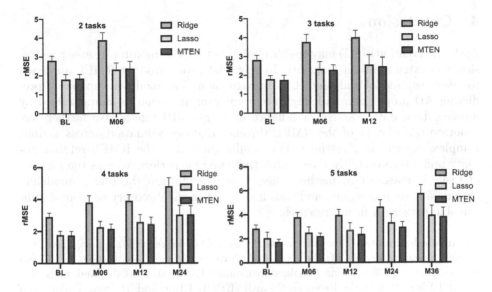

Fig. 3. Histograms of the effect of different numbers of tasks on model performance.

assumption relationship is worth scrutinizing needs to be paid more attention. Therefore, several sets of experiments were designed to test the validity of this relationship. We carried out four sets of experiments using from two to five tasks together to build MTFL model. The purpose of the experiment is to find whether the performance of the model can be improved under a certain task relationship. The results were based on 50 iterations of experiments on different splits of data with 9:1 using 5-fold cross validation. Three algorithms (Ridge, Lasso, MTEN) were conducted in each group for comparison. The results are shown in the Fig. 3. The finding shows that:

- As the number of tasks in MTL increases, the accuracy gains of MTL models in AD progression prediction become more obvious. This proves the effectiveness of multi-task learning.
- At 3 or 4 tasks were considered, the errors of the Lasso and MTEN are small. This may be due to the fact that the core element of structure-based regularization of MTFL is the use of L1norm. Due to the high similarity between tasks, there is thus less complementary information between tasks, i.e., fewer tasks do not yield significant performance gains.
- The discrepancy results is most obvious when the five tasks is considered simultaneously in one model. Result implies that the sharing knowledge between multiple tasks are effective. Noting that the tasks error also increase, this may be due to a non-linear relationship of MRI features and cognitive scores in the late stage of AD progression.

4   Conclusion

Early intervention of AD may enable clinicians to better monitor disease progression and extend patient longevity. In this study, we introduce RMFL approach to effectively model and predict AD progression. The model is capable of predicting AD progression with high accuracy, even in scenarios characterized by missing data, data scarcity, or reliance on single MRI inputs. We further corroborate the efficacy of the RMFL through rigorous validation across various complex experimental settings. The results show that the RMFL retains stability and interpretability while exhibiting superior performance as the number of tasks increases. This method offers new insights into the role of modeling chronic disease progression and thus may assist in the discovery of more significant biomarkers in future research.

Acknowledgements. The authors wish to acknowledge the support from the Young Scientists Fund of the National Natural Science Foundation of China (Grant No.62301452), China Scholarship Council (No.202107030007) and Engineering and Physical Sciences Research Council (EPSRC) Doctoral Training Partnership (EP/T517835/1).

A   Lasso and multi-task lasso

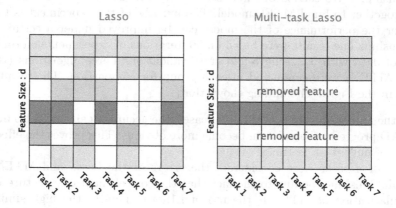

Fig. 4. A comparison of models built by Lasso or a Multi-task Lasso. White block indicates that the parameter value of the position is zero, otherwise, non-zero positions indicated by different colors are used.

B Pipeline

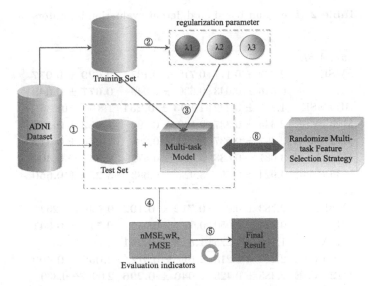

Fig. 5. Pipeline of empirical protocol design.

C Repeated experiments times

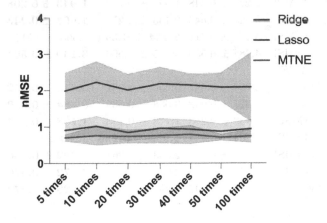

Fig. 6. Evaluation results of repeated experiments times.

D   Evaluation indicators

Table 2. The result based on different evaluation indicators

	Ridge	Lasso	MTEN
cv: nMSE			
nMSE	2.779 ± 0.177	0.718 ± 0.137	**0.629 ± 0.077**
wR	0.516 ± 0.043	0.630 ± 0.049	**0.677 ± 0.049**
BL rMSE	1.805 ± 0.232	**1.803 ± 0.251**	1.816 ± 0.286
M06 rMSE	2.345 ± 0.337	2.132 ± 0.293	**1.962 ± 0.182**
M12 rMSE	2.393 ± 0.537	2.393 ± 0.385	**1.966 ± 0.312**
M24 rMSE	3.087 ± 0.633	3.087 ± 0.572	**2.345 ± 0.400**
M36 rMSE	4.924 ± 0.751	3.924 ± 0.683	**3.232 ± 0.550**
cv: wR			
nMSE	2.783 ± 0.072	**0.712 ± 0.192**	0.750 ± 0.269
wR	0.514 ± 0.050	0.667 ± 0.043	**0.710 ± 0.041**
BL rMSE	1.702 ± 0.225	**1.813 ± 0.291**	2.112 ± 0.329
M06 rMSE	2.293 ± 0.218	2.109 ± 0.312	**2.059 ± 0.309**
M12 rMSE	2.385 ± 0.425	**2.040 ± 0.296**	2.092 ± 0.330
M24 rMSE	3.975 ± 0.648	**2.570 ± 0.470**	2.579 ± 0.809
M36 rMSE	4.635 ± 0.577	3.741 ± 1.118	**3.528 ± 0.888**
cv: rMSE			
nMSE	2.788 ± 0.091	0.684 ± 0.194	**0.630 ± 0.007**
wR	0.522 ± 0.044	0.648 ± 0.062	**0.691 ± 0.042**
BL rMSE	1.776 ± 0.229	**1.823 ± 0.293**	1.879 ± 0.277
M06 rMSE	2.275 ± 0.348	1.996 ± 0.262	**1.943 ± 0.208**
M12 rMSE	3.523 ± 0.543	2.133 ± 0.272	**1.907 ± 0.243**
M24 rMSE	4.180 ± 0.411	**2.424 ± 0.544**	2.563 ± 0.515
M36 rMSE	4.788 ± 0.556	3.345 ± 0.596	**3.149 ± 0.584**
cv: MSE			
nMSE	2.765 ± 0.057	0.650 ± 0.087	**0.613 ± 0.132**
wR	0.527 ± 0.032	0.658 ± 0.039	**0.684 ± 0.039**
BL rMSE	1.806 ± 0.218	1.748 ± 0.148	**1.738 ± 0.252**
M06 rMSE	2.304 ± 0.354	**1.952 ± 0.234**	2.059 ± 0.267
M12 rMSE	2.338 ± 0.486	2.083 ± 0.261	**1.992 ± 0.236**
M24 rMSE	3.138 ± 0.759	2.689 ± 0.541	**2.472 ± 0.576**
M36 rMSE	3.876 ± 0.597	3.391 ± 0.645	**3.228 ± 0.579**

References

1. Association, A.: 2019 Alzheimer's disease facts and figures. Alzheimer Dement. **15**(3), 321–387 (2019)
2. Breiman, L.: Arcing classifiers. Tech. rep., Technical report, University of California, Department of Statistics (1996)
3. Chakravorti, T., Satyanarayana, P.: Non linear system identification using kernel based exponentially extended random vector functional link network. Appl. Soft Comput. **89**, 106117 (2020)
4. Fischl, B.: Freesurfer. Neuroimage **62**(2), 774–781 (2012)
5. Ghazi, M.M., et al.: Training recurrent neural networks robust to incomplete data: application to Alzheimer's disease progression modeling. Med. Image Anal. **53**, 39–46 (2019)
6. Gong, P., Ye, J., Zhang, C.s.: Multi-stage multi-task feature learning. In: Advances in Neural Information Processing Systems 25 (2012)
7. Ito, K., et al.: Disease progression model for cognitive deterioration from Alzheimer's disease neuroimaging initiative database. Alzheimer. Dement. **7**(2), 151–160 (2011)
8. Khachaturian, Z.S.: Diagnosis of Alzheimer's disease. Arch. Neurol. **42**(11), 1097–1105 (1985)
9. Liu, K., Wang, R.: Antisaturation adaptive fixed-time sliding mode controller design to achieve faster convergence rate and its application. IEEE Trans. Circuits Syst. II Exp. Briefs **69**(8), 3555–3559 (2022)
10. Liu, K., Yang, P., Wang, R., Jiao, L., Li, T., Zhang, J.: Observer-based adaptive fuzzy finite-time attitude control for quadrotor UAVs. IEEE Trans. Aerosp. Electron. Syst. (2023)
11. Nguyen, M.: Predicting Alzheimer's disease progression using deep recurrent neural networks. Neuroimage **222**, 117203 (2020)
12. Peng, J., Zhu, X., Wang, Y., An, L., Shen, D.: Structured sparsity regularized multiple kernel learning for Alzheimer's disease diagnosis. Pattern Recogn. **88**, 370–382 (2019)
13. Rao, C., Liu, M., Goh, M., Wen, J.: 2-stage modified random forest model for credit risk assessment of p2p network lending to "three rurals" borrowers. Appl. Soft Comput. **95**, 106570 (2020)
14. Stonnington, C.M., et al.: Predicting clinical scores from magnetic resonance scans in Alzheimer's disease. Neuroimage **51**(4), 1405–1413 (2010)
15. Sun, M., Baytas, I.M., Zhan, L., Wang, Z., Zhou, J.: Subspace network: deep multi-task censored regression for modeling neurodegenerative diseases. In: Proceedings of the 24th ACM SIGKDD International Conference on Knowledge Discovery & Data Mining, pp. 2259–2268 (2018)
16. Utkin, L.V., Kovalev, M.S., Coolen, F.P.: Imprecise weighted extensions of random forests for classification and regression. Appl. Soft Comput. **92**, 106324 (2020)
17. Wang, G., Ma, J., Chen, G., Yang, Y.: Financial distress prediction: regularized sparse-based random subspace with ER aggregation rule incorporating textual disclosures. Appl. Soft Comput. **90**, 106152 (2020)
18. Wang, S., Wang, Y., Wang, D., Yin, Y., Wang, Y., Jin, Y.: An improved random forest-based rule extraction method for breast cancer diagnosis. Appl. Soft Comput. **86**, 105941 (2020)
19. Wang, X., Qi, J., Yang, Y., Yang, P.: A survey of disease progression modeling techniques for Alzheimer's diseases. In: 2019 IEEE 17th International Conference on Industrial Informatics (INDIN), vol. 1, pp. 1237–1242. IEEE (2019)

20. Yang, P., Bi, G., Qi, J., Wang, X., Yang, Y., Xu, L.: Multimodal wearable intelligence for dementia care in healthcare 4.0: a survey. Inf. Syst. Front. 1–18
21. Yang, P., et al.: Feasibility study of mitigation and suppression intervention strategies for controlling Covid-19 outbreaks in London and Wuhan (2020)
22. Yang, P., Yang, C., Lanfranchi, V., Ciravegna, F.: Activity graph based convolutional neural network for human activity recognition using acceleration and gyroscope data. IEEE Trans. Ind. Inf. **18**(10), 6619–6630 (2022)
23. Yang, P., et al.: DUAPM: an effective dynamic micro-blogging user activity prediction model towards cyber-physical-social systems. IEEE Trans. Ind. Inf. **16**(8), 5317–5326 (2019)
24. Zhang, Y., Lanfranchi, V., Wang, X., Zhou, M., Yang, P.: Modeling Alzheimer's disease progression via amalgamated magnitude-direction brain structure variation quantification and tensor multi-task learning. In: 2022 IEEE International Conference on Bioinformatics and Biomedicine (BIBM), pp. 2735–2742. IEEE (2022)
25. Zhou, J., Yuan, L., Liu, J., Ye, J.: A multi-task learning formulation for predicting disease progression. In: Proceedings of the 17th ACM SIGKDD International Conference on Knowledge Discovery and Data Mining, pp. 814–822 (2011)
26. Zhou, M., Zhang, Y., Yang, Y., Liu, T., Yang, P.: Robust temporal smoothness in multi-task learning. In: Proceedings of the AAAI Conference on Artificial Intelligence, vol. 37, pp. 11426–11434 (2023)

Adaptive Prior Correction in Alzheimer's Disease Spatio-Temporal Modeling via Multi-task Learning

Xiangchao Chang[1], Menghui Zhou[2], Yun Yang[1], and Po Yang[2(✉)]

[1] Yunnan University, Kunming, China
yangyun@ynu.edu.cn
[2] University of Sheffield, Sheffield, UK
po.yang@sheffield.ac.uk

Abstract. Multi-task learning methods have been studied in Alzheimer's disease for cognitive status prediction and neuroimaging feature identification widely by utilizing prior constraints. However, the existing models do not explicitly model the spatio-temporal connectivity for the lack of samples and prior medical knowledge. In this article, we propose a sparse multi-task learning model for cognitive status prediction, which is adaptively weighted in sparse prior to prevent the error in spatial feature correlation learning, and incorporated with prior domain knowledge to estimate the progression with adaptive correction. Inference in our spatio-temporal model is based on majorization-minimization optimization guaranteed convergence properties. The proposed model is applied to a real-world neuroimaging study to predict cognitive tests scores and structured feature mining with MRI scans. The effectiveness of the proposed progression model is demonstrated by its superior prediction performance over multiple competing methods and accurate identification of compact sets of cognition-relevant biomarkers.

Keywords: Alzheimer's Disease · Multi-task Learning · Constrained Optimization

1 Introduction

Alzheimer' Disease (AD), a severe neurodegenerative disorder, causes a heavy financial burden on society, with an estimated global annual cost of US$1 trillion [3]. Predicting the status of patients helped in clinical settings, such as informing diagnosis, prognosis, and treatment planning, and identifying neuroimaging predictors [6, 21]. Some data-oriented methods seek to help inferring AD patients' cognitive and functional status from neuroimaging biomarkers from individual magnetic resonance imaging (MRI) or positron emission tomography (PET) of brain tissues and possible risk factors such as age, gender years of education, and ApoE gene in [11, 22, 28, 36, 38, 39]. However, several existing models do not make a precise prediction for the longitudinal prediction of months or years forecast, due to the neglect of temporal connectivity of disease progression.

J. Qi and P. Yang (Eds.): IoTBDH 2023, CCIS 2019, pp. 69–83, 2024.
https://doi.org/10.1007/978-3-031-52216-1_6

Multi-task learning (MTL) is a machine learning framework, utilized the intrinsic relationship among related tasks to leverage generation performance [5,30]. It has been commonly used to obtain better generation performance and make a medium or long-term forecast of patients' cognitive status rather than single-task learning [38,39]. For the reason of ambiguous pathology of Alzheimer's disease, some sparsity-inducing properties employed for process-related features mining among large-scale of latent pathogenic features, for instance, LASSO [18] is widely used in feature weight shrinkage with a sparse prior distribution constraint. In [11,38,39], fused LASSO was used for feature selection in an inhomogeneous way for single task and overall tasks. [28] proposed a sparse Bayesian MTL approach, applied in the multiple measurement vector model to learn sparse correlation both in prior distribution and optimization stages. Past several methods identified neuroimaging biomarkers by sparse prior over features, neglected the sparse prior over features relationship.

Spatial feature connectivity learning can help researchers to identify the relational features of processes [10,35]. Learning feature connectivity by the Gaussian graphical model to describe the feature networks is a straight approach in relevant studies [9,34]. In [9], a brain connectivity learning model with sparse inverse covariance estimation was proposed based on PET data. Three stages of AD progression were taken into account to clarify the differences and changes in the connectivity model as the disease progresses. Besides, [33] proposed a feature extractor based on the Gaussian graphical model to classify AD individuals. Both of them employed the structural prior knowledge among biomarkers extracted from neuroimages, which may lose accuracy than identification from the structure pre-selected as disease relevant [8]. To obtain a sparse solution in feature connectivity learning, sparsity priors like LASSO [18] are used widely as a replacement of l_0 norm with a convex formulation. However, larger coefficients are penalized more heavily in the l_1 norm than smaller coefficients [4]. The imbalance of penalisation among the spatial features causes the deviation in connectivity learning, especially in the calculation of the correlation matrix.

The focus of the current articles is on MTL of AD, where tasks involve better general performance by predicting a set of cognitive scores over multiple time points, and each task focuses on each checked time points of patients. The prediction performance for each subtask is influenced by the cognitive status measurements error and shows fluctuation in AD longitudinal study. In [38,39], adjacent time points prediction tasks residual error estimator proposed based on medical prior knowledge that multiple regression models from different time points satisfy the smoothness property [40,41] while neglecting the complicated progression of all time points. Global residual error constraints have been learned in [11,36,38], formulated the task correlation by prior knowledge. A Laplacian matrix (or Nadaraya-Watson kernel) constraint is proposed in [11] to make a global smoothness constraint with adjustable bandwidth to control the smoothness region among time points. Considering the dynamical process of AD, [40] utilized a automatic method to simulate disease progression asymmetrical correlation among prediction tasks. Besides the prior knowledge, [36] learned the spatio-temporal similarity or disease progression by correlation analysis according to the data, while the small quantity of instances in AD research would lose the accuracy in connectivity learning. However, the ambiguous pathogenesis research on AD causes a big challenge to model the disease progression exactly.

In this article, we propose a new spatio-temporal multi-task learning model, for modeling the AD progression and feature connectivity learning with adaptive prior correction, highlighting the following contributions:

- We propose a multi-task sparse feature correlation learning method based on Gaussian graphical model with a more democratic penalization to overcome the effect of convex sparse prior in correlation estimation.
- We formulate a new longitudinal dependency constraint in Alzheimer's disease process estimation. The constraint penalty could fix prior medical knowledge temporal simulation deficiency in disease process estimation by data intrinsic characteristics.
- Our model shows superior interpretability and accuracy in both cognitive status prediction tasks and structural feature mining of AD in MRI imaging study from the Alzheimer's Disease Neuroimaging Initiative (ADNI) database compared with multiple competing methods.

The rest of the article is organized as follows. In Sect. 2, we present our disease progression model based MTL, and give an optimization method. In Sect. 3, we present experiment results on ADNI data and make an explanation of selected features with former medical research. The conclusion and future directions are given in Sect. 4.

2   Methodology

In this section, we describe the formulation of our spatio-temporal adaptive prior correction progression model (STAC). First, we propose a sparsity adaptive correction method (SAC), followed by a temporal relation adaptive correction (TAC) process estimator in Alzheimer's Disease progression, then we give an optimization method of our formulation by alternative directions method of multipliers algorithm.

2.1   Sparsity Adaptive Correction in Spatial Feature Connectivity Learning

Gaussian graphical model [2] in our feature connectivity learning can be demonstrated as: a $d-$dimension random vector sets $r = (r_1, r_2, ..., r_n)$ with joint distribution Z. An undirected graph $G = (V, E)$ characterized Z by the vertex set V represents the d covariates of r, and edge set E represents the conditional dependence relations between the covariates of r. Assuming $r \sim N(0, \Sigma)$, if r_i and r_j is conditionally independent, the inverse covariance matrix $\Omega(i, j) = 0$, where the $\Omega = \Sigma^{-1}$. And the empirical covariance matrix is $\hat{\Sigma} = \frac{1}{n} \sum_{i=1}^{n} (r_i - \bar{r})^T (r_i - \bar{r})$, where $\bar{r}$ denotes the mean of samples. Because the sparsity of Alzheimer's Disease instances and features, multi-task learning model could leverage the domain-specific information contained in training samples of correlational tasks [5]. In our sparse feature correlation learning, we assume that each row $\hat{w}_i$ of the weight matrix W follows a multivariate Gaussian distribution with zero mean and precision matrix Ω, where $\Omega = \Sigma^{-1}$, and $\hat{w}_i \sim N(0, \Sigma)$. The posterior can be written as follow for a multivariate Gaussian prior over features:

$$P(W|X, Y; \Omega) \propto \prod_{t=1}^{T} \prod_{i=1}^{n_t} P(y_t^{(i)}|x_t^{(i)}, w_t) \prod_{j=1}^{d} P(\hat{w}_j|\Omega) \tag{1}$$

where $y_t \in R^n$ is the response for the t–th tasks, regressed on the data matrix $X_t \in R^{n*d}$ with n samples and dimension d. In the cognitive status prediction of AD progression model, X denotes the neuroimaging measures of patients, Y denotes the cognitive tests score of corresponding patients in corresponding time points; where the first term on the right-hand side denotes the conditional distribution of the response given the input and parameters, and the second term denotes the prior over rows of W. We build our spatial feature connectivity model by the constraint that the learned structure must contribute to cognitive status prediction tasks. The optimization problem of (1) could be solved by minimization of the negative logarithm of (1), corresponding to a linear regression problem with regularization as follows:

$$\underset{W}{argmin} \frac{1}{2} \sum_{t=1}^{T} ||X_t * w_t - y_t||_2^2 - \frac{d}{2} log|\Omega| + Tr(W^T \Omega W) \tag{2}$$

where $|\cdot|$ denotes the determinant. A sparse prior knowledge over Ω and W caused by Alzheimer's Disease unknown etiology can be applied in (2) to select relational biomarkers:

$$\begin{aligned} \underset{W}{argmin} \frac{1}{2} \sum_{t=1}^{T} ||X_t * w_t - y_t||_2^2 - \frac{d}{2} log|\Omega| \\ + Tr(W^T \Omega W) + \lambda_1 ||\Omega||_1 + \lambda_2 ||W||_{rl_1} \end{aligned} \tag{3}$$

where $||\cdot||_1$ denotes l_1 norm [18] as a sparse inducer, is widely used as an approximation of l_0 norm, which is an np-hard problem. And $||\cdot||_{rl_1}$ denotes $reweighted - l_1$ norm in [4] with the formulation of $log(|\cdot| + \epsilon), \epsilon > 0$. The enhancing sparsity property can be illustrated that the log-sum penalty function is better than traditional convex l_1 relaxation in l_0 norm approximate solution [4]. However, the concave penalty brings a challenge in optimization, we illustrate the adaptive weight adjustment property by iterative optimization algorithm based on Majorization-Minimization as:

– 1. Set the iteration count c to zero and weighted matrix

$$Q_{i,j}^{(0)} = 1, i = 1, ..., d, j = 1, ..., T.$$

- 2. Solve the weighted $l_1 - norm$ minimization problem, where $\odot$ denotes the Hadamard product,

$$W^{(c)} = argmin\|Q^{(c)} \odot W\|_1$$

- 3. Update the weights: for each $c = 1, ..., n$

$$Q_{i,j}^{(c+1)} = \frac{1}{|W_{i,j}^{(c)}| + \epsilon}$$

- 4. Terminate on convergence or when c attains a specified maximum number of iterations c_{max}. Otherwise, increment c and go to step 2.

With an iterative reweighted optimization, the $reweighted-l_1$ norm provides a heterogeneous constraint in the regression parameter matrix, to eliminate the bias of learning connectivity by data from different ranges and dimensions.

2.2 Temporal Relation Adaptive Correction

The critical issues in multi-task learning are to identify how the tasks are related and build learning models to capture such relatedness with different prior knowledge [37,41]. In Alzheimer's Disease progression study, the cognitive scores of patients presented fluctuation in varying degrees, although the treatment can delay the disease to some extent, it is different from the medical theory that AD caused irreversible cognitive function damage. Considering the temporal smoothness of the cognitive status of patients, local or global smoothness penalized regularization in [11,38] showed good performance in prediction tasks. An accurate identification of AD process needs more prior knowledge in medicine, so we proposed a marginal distribution constraint that allowed prior knowledge to be incorporated into the process estimation with adaptive correction.

Concentrating on the fluctuation of patients' cognitive scores, a constraint on adjacent time points cognitive scores difference by $\Delta y = y_t - y_{t+1} = Xw_t - Xw_{t+1} = X(w_t - w_{t+1})$. Considering the columns of the weight matrix w_t, each of them presents a predicted task of a time point. Our MTL formulations focus on encouraging sparsity on the residual error: $\gamma_t = w_t - \hat{w}_t = w_t - \sum_{l=1, l \neq t}^{T} r_{l,t} w_l$ $t = 1, .., T$. Where r is entries of correlation matrix R identified the correlation of tasks.

$$\Gamma = WR = \begin{bmatrix} \gamma_1 \\ \gamma_2 \\ \vdots \\ \gamma_t \end{bmatrix}^T = \begin{bmatrix} w_1 \\ w_2 \\ \vdots \\ w_t \end{bmatrix}^T \begin{bmatrix} 1 & -r_{1,2} & -r_{1,3} & \cdots & -r_{1,T} \\ -r_{2,1} & 1 & -r_{2,3} & \cdots & -r_{2,T} \\ \vdots & \vdots & \vdots & \ddots & \vdots \\ -r_{T,1} & -r_{T,2} & -r_{T,3} & \cdots & 1 \end{bmatrix}$$

Considering a 'perfect' correlation matrix R, it means that relationships between multiple tasks of the same feature parameter are completely decoupled. $\gamma \sim \mathcal{N}(\mu, \tau^{-1})$ and conjugate prior $Gam(\tau|a, b)$. Calculate the Gaussian marginal distribution as:

$$p(\gamma|\mu,a,b) = \int_0^\infty \mathcal{N}(\gamma|\mu,\tau^{-1})Gam(\tau|a,b)d\tau$$

$$= \frac{b^a}{Gamma(a)}(\frac{1}{2\pi})^{\frac{1}{2}}[b+\frac{(\gamma-\mu)^2}{2}]^{-a-\frac{1}{2}} Gamma(a+\frac{1}{2})$$

(4)

Noticed that Gam denotes the Gamma distribution, and $Gamma$ denotes the Gamma function. It should be separated from residual error matrix Γ and its elements γ. Assuming that γ follows a zero-mean distribution, the formula 4 can be transformed as:

$$PDF(\gamma) = \frac{1}{\sqrt{v}B(\frac{1}{2},\frac{v}{2})}(1+\frac{\gamma^2}{v})^{-(v+1)/2}$$

where PDF is the short for probability density function, $v = 2a$ is the degrees of freedom, B denotes the $Beta$ function. The maximum posterior estimate of residual error γ can be written as negative logarithm as: $log(\gamma^2+\epsilon)$, $\epsilon > 0$. So the constraint of residual error is $log(\gamma_i^2+\epsilon)$. To solve the concavity optimization of log function, we consider the upper bound by:

$$log(\gamma_i^2+\epsilon) \le \frac{\gamma_i^2+\epsilon}{\varrho} + log(\varrho) - 1$$

where $\varrho \ge 0$ is arbitrary, the right hand side of inequality becomes equality when $\varrho = \gamma_i^2 + \epsilon$. Now consider solving the convex optimization problem $\sum_i \frac{\gamma_i^2+\epsilon}{\varrho} + log(\varrho)$, for fixed ϵ, ϱ, the optimal Γ is easy to solve by analytical solution. The minimizing ϱ for fixed Γ, ϵ is $\varrho = \gamma_i^2 + \epsilon$, so the concave penalty can be solved by the iterative algorithm via the construction upon.

The marginal distribution constraints can be seen as $reweighted - l_2$ in [23] extended to progression estimation. Elementwise marginal distribution could reduce the impact of changes in different scales of features, meanwhile, the adaptive parameter constraint will help both in the correction of the prior correlation matrix and enhancing sparsity in multi-stages.

Combined with the sparsity adaptive correction in spatial feature connectivity learning, our spatio-temporal adaptive prior correction learning model (STAC) is:

$$L_\rho(W,\Omega,\Gamma,V) = \frac{1}{2}\sum_{t=1}^T ||X_t * w_t - y_t||_2^2 - \frac{d}{2}log|\Omega| + Tr(W^T\Omega W)$$

$$+ \lambda_1||\Omega||_1 + \lambda_2||W||_{rl_1} + \lambda_3||W||_{2,1} + \lambda_4||\Gamma||_{rl_2}$$

(5)

$$s.t. \ WR = \Gamma$$

2.3 Optimization of Sparse Spatial Feature Connectivity with Progression Adaptive-Correction Learning Model

In this section, we illustrate the method to solve the optimization problem 5 due to the non-smooth, concave, and coupling terms. We propose an iterative optimization algorithm based on the alternative directions method of multipliers method (ADMM) [2]. ADMM could solve the global optimization problem as alternative updating local subproblems. The alternating algorithm proceeds as follows:

The augmented Lagrangian function is:

$$L(W, \Omega, \Gamma, V) = \frac{1}{2} \sum_{t=1}^{T} ||X_t * w_t - y_t||_2^2 - \frac{d}{2} log|\Omega| + Tr(W^T \Omega W)$$
$$+ \lambda_1 ||\Omega||_1 + \lambda_2 ||W||_{rl1} + \lambda_3 ||W||_{2,1} + \lambda_4 ||\Gamma||_{rl_2}$$
$$+ Tr(V^T(WR - \Gamma)) + \frac{\rho}{2} ||WR - \Gamma||_2^2$$

where V is the Lagrangian multiplier corresponding to the constraints $WR = \Gamma$, and $\rho > 0$ is penalty effectively determining the step size for dual ascent in ADMM. For iteration index i, the updates of $W_{i+1}, \Omega_{i+1}, \Gamma_{i+1}$ can be solved by the fixed W_i, Ω_i, Γ_i, and a detailed illustration is as follow.

$$\underset{W}{argmin} \frac{1}{2} \sum_{t=1}^{T} ||X_t * w_t - y_t||_2^2 + Tr(W^T \Omega W) + \lambda_2 ||W||_{rl_1}$$
$$+ \lambda_3 ||W||_{2,1} + Tr(V^T(WR - \Gamma)) + \frac{\rho}{2} ||WR - \Gamma||_2^2 \qquad (6)$$

We solve the subproblem with concave penalty $reweighted - l_1$ norm of $\lambda_2 ||W||_{rl_1}$ with the Nesterov accelerating method [13], and detailed described in Sect. 2.1. The update step for Ω, is known as sparse inverse covariance selection (SICS) problem [2,20] as:

$$\underset{\Omega}{argmin} \, Tr(W^T \Omega W) - \frac{d}{2} log|\Omega| + \lambda_1 ||\Omega||_1 \qquad (7)$$

To solve the problem 7, we utilized the proximal point algorithm in [27], and it can be accelerated with FISTA [1] or Nesterov [13] accelerated gradient descent with strong convexity of constructed function:

$$x^{k+1} = prox_{t_k \psi}(x^k) = \underset{u}{argmin}\{\psi(u) + \frac{1}{2t_k} ||u - x^k||_2^2\}$$

We consider the problem 7 by introducing variable Υ, and transformed as:

$$\underset{\Omega, \Upsilon}{min} \, \psi(\Omega, \Upsilon) = -\frac{d}{2} log|\Omega| + <S, \Omega> + \lambda_1 ||\Upsilon||_1 + I_D(\Omega, \Upsilon)$$

where $D = \{(\Omega, \Upsilon) | \Omega - \Upsilon = 0\}$, $S = WW^T$, $< \cdot, \cdot >$ denotes the inner product. I_D is the index function of the set D. And we solve the problem as follows in $k-$th step iteration by proximal point algorithm:

$$\min_{\Omega, \Upsilon} \psi(\Omega, \Upsilon) + \frac{1}{2t_k}(||\Omega - \Omega^k||_F^2 + ||\Upsilon - \Upsilon^k||_F^2) \tag{8}$$

We introduce the multiplier Z to construct the dual function to solve the problem 8.

$$\Phi_k(Z) = \inf_{\Omega}\{-\frac{d}{2}log|\Omega| + <Z, \Omega> + \frac{1}{2t_k}(||\Omega - \Omega^k||_F^2\}$$

$$+ \inf_{\Upsilon}\{\lambda_1||\Upsilon||_1 + <S - Z, \Upsilon> + \frac{1}{2t_k}||\Upsilon - \Upsilon^k||_F^2\}$$

$$= \Xi_{tk}^1(\Omega^k - t_k Z) - \frac{1}{2t_k}(||\Omega - t_k Z||_F^2 - ||\Omega||_F^2)$$

$$+ \lambda_1\Xi_{\lambda_1 t_k}^2(\Upsilon^k - t_k(S - Z)) - \frac{1}{2t_k}(||\Upsilon^k - t_k(S - Z)||_F^2 - ||\Upsilon||_F^2),$$

$$\Xi_{t_k}^1(A) = \inf_{\Omega}\{-\frac{d}{2}log|\Omega| + \frac{1}{2t_k}||\Omega - A||_F^2\},$$

$$\Xi_{\lambda_1 t_k}^2(B) = \inf_{\Upsilon}\{||\Upsilon||_1 + \frac{1}{2\lambda_1 t_k}||\Upsilon - B||_2^2\}$$

For the symmetry matrix A, eigenvalue decomposition is $A = Q\Lambda Q^T$, and $QQ^T = Q^TQ = I$, $\Lambda = diag(\Lambda_1, ..., \Lambda_n)$. Define:

$$q_{t_k}^+(c) = \frac{1}{2}(\sqrt{c^2 + 4t_k} + c), q_{t_k}^-(c) = \frac{1}{2}(\sqrt{c^2 + 4t_k} + c), c \in R,$$

$$A^+ = Qdiag(q_{t_k}^+(\Lambda_1), q_{t_k}^+(\Lambda_2), ..., q_{t_k}^+(\Lambda_n))Q^T,$$

$$A^- = Qdiag(q_{t_k}^-(\Lambda_1), q_{t_k}^-(\Lambda_2), ..., q_{t_k}^-(\Lambda_n))Q^T.$$

The gradient of $\Xi_{t_k}^1(A)$ is $\nabla_A\Xi_{t_k}^1(A) = A - A^+$, and the minimum of $\Xi_{t_k}^1(A)$ is got when $\Omega = A^+$, $\Xi_{t_k}^1(A) = -\frac{t_k d}{2}log|\Omega| + \frac{1}{2}||A^-||_F^2$. And the $\Xi_{\lambda_1 t_k}^2(B)$ can be solved as the proximal gradient algorithm of LASSO [14], with the gradient of $\nabla_B\Xi_{\lambda_1 t_k}^2(B) = \frac{1}{\lambda_1 t_k}(B - prox_{\lambda_1 t_k||\cdot||_1}(B))$. So the proximal gradient algorithm of problem 7 in $k-$th step iteration is:

$$Z^{k+1} \approx \underset{Z}{argmax}\ \Phi_k(Z) - \frac{1}{t_k}||Z - Z^k||_F^2$$

$$\Omega^{k+1} = prox_{-\frac{t_k d}{2}log|\cdot|}(\Omega^k - t_k Z^{k+1}) \tag{9}$$

$$\Upsilon^{k+1} = prox_{\lambda_1 t_k||\cdot||_1}(\Upsilon^k - t_k(S - Z^{k+1}))$$

Noticed that we utilize the dual function to minus the proximal component to ensure strong concavity, because the $\Phi_k(Z)$ is not strongly concave. The update of Γ is as follow function with a closed form solution.

$$\underset{\Gamma}{argmin}\ \lambda_4||\Gamma||_{rl_2} + Tr(V^T(WR - \Gamma)) + \frac{\rho}{2}||WR - \Gamma||_2^2 \tag{10}$$

The penalty $reweighted - l_2$ norm can be written as $M \odot ||W||^2$, M is the weight matrix of $reweighted - l_2$ norm, and update in each iteration counts i by $m^{(i+1)} = \frac{1}{|m^{(i)}|^2 + \epsilon_2}$, where m denotes the entries of M, $\epsilon_2 > 0$ is the parameter of iterative algorithm. The dual variable V is updated as ADMM dual variable ascending method. The main cause in the complexity of our algorithms is the eigenvalue decomposition in Ω updating steps and can be optimized by parallel computing during the update process.

3   Experiments

In this section, we present experimental analysis to demonstrate the effectiveness of the proposed framework on characterizing AD spatial feature connectivity and adaptive correction progression estimation using a dataset from ADNI [31].

3.1   Experimental Setting

In our work, we apply empirical evaluation to longitudinal progression studies of MRI data. The biomarkers are based on MRI data from ADNI, and processed by FreeSurfer image analysis suite by UCSF (University of California, San Francisco). We removed features with over 1000 missing entries and patients with no baseline records. And 314 MRI features could be grouped into the following categories: average cortical thickness, standard deviation in cortical thickness, the volumes of cortical parcellations, the volumes of specific white matter parcellations, and the total surface area of the cortex. Three kinds of cognitive test scores were used in our model training target: Alzheimer's Disease Assessment Scale cognitive Subscale (ADAS-cog) [7], Mini Mental State Examination (MMSE) [19] and Rey's Auditory Verbal Learning Test (RAVLT) [24] The RAVLT includes TOTAL (total score of the first 5 learning trials), TOT6 (trial 6 total number of words recalled) and T30 (30 min delay total number of words recalled).

For the quantitative performance evaluation, we employ the metrics of the normalized mean squared error (nMSE), weighted R-value (WR) for aggregated performance over all time points. And root mean squared error (rMSE) for the single time point evaluation. We split the data into training sets and testing sets by 9:1, and 20 trials with 5-fold cross-validation performed to select the best hyperparameter $(\lambda_1, \lambda_2, \lambda_3, \lambda_4)$, and use the selected hyperparameter to make prediction in test sets. The regularization parameters are chosen from a log scale of 10^{-2} to 10^3, and the iterative reweighted algorithms parameters ϵ_1 and ϵ_2 are chose from a log scale of 10^{-3} to 10^2.

In terms of progression model performance, we compared our method with different multi-task regression methods. A multi-task regression model based on sparse Gaussian graph model (MSSL) in [8] was chosen to compare our sparsity adaptive correction method (SAC). Besides, we chose AD progression model with parameter sharing mechanism and disease progression prior constraints cFSGL [38] and FL-SGL [11] as competing methods. We employed two temporal prior correlation matrices as temporal relation adaptive correction learning method with local smoothness constraint of coherent column residual (TAC-L). And temporal relation adaptive correction learning method with global smoothness constraint based Nadaraya-Watson kernel estimator (TAC-G), and incorporated with the SAC as STAC-L and STAC-G. For the comparison of spatio-temporal adaptive prior correction, we choose a Multiple-output Regression with Output and Task Structures (MROTS) in [16]. The average and standard deviation of performance measures are calculated by 20 iterations of trails on different splits of data, shown in Tables 1, 2. Because of the lack of space, we show the prediction performance of each time points on MMSE and ADAS in Fig. 1.

Table 1. Prediction performance comparison of models in terms of nMSE (lower is better). 90% of data is used as training data, and shown data in this table is mean value ± standard derivation.

Method	MMSE	ADAS	TOTAL	TOT6	TOT30
MSSL	2.701 ± 0.263	5.937 ± 0.336	2.262 ± 0.086	2.920 ± 0.129	3.110 ± 0.092
SAC	2.600 ± 0.255	5.814 ± 0.274	2.312 ± 0.104	2.866 ± 0.132	2.872 ± 0.105
CFSGL	2.495 ± 0.167	5.598 ± 0.374	2.190 ± 0.115	2.727 ± 0.130	2.809 ± 0.106
FL-SGL	2.310 ± 0.115	5.617 ± 0.394	2.153 ± 0.103	2.668 ± 0.081	2.856 ± 0.137
TAC-L	2.415 ± 0.157	5.577 ± 0.333	2.147 ± 0.097	$\mathbf{2.237 \pm 0.109}$	$\mathbf{2.737 \pm 0.144}$
TAC-G	2.501 ± 0.199	5.593 ± 0.294	2.184 ± 0.111	2.546 ± 0.099	2.774 ± 0.176
MROTS	2.752 ± 0.276	5.600 ± 0.303	2.144 ± 0.068	2.520 ± 0.116	2.883 ± 0.087
STAC-L	2.351 ± 0.110	$\mathbf{5.538 \pm 0.376}$	2.145 ± 0.076	2.601 ± 0.122	2.809 ± 0.106
STAC-G	$\mathbf{2.220 \pm 0.111}$	5.632 ± 0.438	$\mathbf{2.138 \pm 0.112}$	2.670 ± 0.138	2.760 ± 0.108

Table 2. Prediction performance comparison of models in terms of wR (higher is better). 90% of data is used as training data, and shown data in this table is mean value ± standard derivation.

Method	MMSE	ADAS	TOTAL	TOT6	TOT30
MSSL	0.601 ± 0.037	0.700 ± 0.025	0.619 ± 0.019	0.592 ± 0.026	0.566 ± 0.016
SAC	0.599 ± 0.026	0.722 ± 0.057	0.646 ± 0.018	0.595 ± 0.035	0.595 ± 0.013
CFSGL	0.648 ± 0.028	0.728 ± 0.021	0.636 ± 0.027	0.615 ± 0.022	0.618 ± 0.020
FL-SGL	0.652 ± 0.017	0.717 ± 0.023	0.637 ± 0.023	0.638 ± 0.020	0.638 ± 0.024
TAC-L	0.660 ± 0.021	0.725 ± 0.020	0.651 ± 0.022	0.645 ± 0.016	0.627 ± 0.024
TAC-G	0.657 ± 0.013	0.719 ± 0.026	$\mathbf{0.671 \pm 0.018}$	0.625 ± 0.036	0.630 ± 0.016
MROTS	0.671 ± 0.025	0.741 ± 0.028	0.619 ± 0.017	0.612 ± 0.031	0.641 ± 0.018
STAC-L	$\mathbf{0.679 \pm 0.015}$	$\mathbf{0.745 \pm 0.031}$	0.657 ± 0.027	$\mathbf{0.650 \pm 0.020}$	0.649 ± 0.016
STAC-G	0.667 ± 0.017	0.744 ± 0.026	0.654 ± 0.024	0.650 ± 0.024	$\mathbf{0.654 \pm 0.030}$

The results shown in Tables 1, 2 and Fig. 1 indicated our adaptive prior correction model make a better performance in cognitive status prediction tasks, which demonstrates the advantage of proposed prior correction in feature connectivity learning and disease progression modeling. While the spatio-temporal adaptive prior correction model with global smoothness constraint in our experiments did not show an absolute advantage over adjacent temporal smoothness constraint, for the following reasons.

- Prediction tasks between long time intervals keep a weakened relationship, caused by several months or even years of the disease process.
- STAC model provides an adaptive constraint in temporal smoothness residual error estimator, and it will enhance the accuracy of modeling the disease progression, meanwhile adjusting temporal structure constraint adaptively.
- Due to the undefined etiology and pathogenesis of AD, the kernel smoothness estimator could not make an explicit description of disease progression.

The later tasks show worse prediction performance caused by many patients dropping out from ADNI study thus the number of samples decreases with the passage of time.

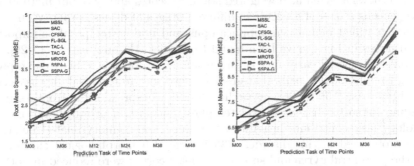

Fig. 1. Prediction performance comparison of each time point in terms of rMSE (lower is better). The left plot is conducted on MMSE dataset and the right plot on ADAS dataset.

3.2   Identification of Structural Longitudinal MRI Biomarkers

We study the identification of temporal biomarkers by longitudinal stability selection in [11,38], with numerous random subsets experiments and computing the frequency of each feature was selected across the tasks for each cognitive status tests. We performed longitudinal stability selection from baseline (M00) to 120 months after baseline (M120). Due to the lack of space, we only show the stability vector for ADAS-Cog and MMSE with top 25 stable features in Fig. 2. SV of Left Hippocampus is shown a high correlation with disease progression in both of cognitive tests of all time. In MMSE tests, a small set of biomarkers was identified, including TA of right precentral, TA of left middle temporal, TA of right entorhinal, and TA of right inferior parietal. TA of left middle temporal,

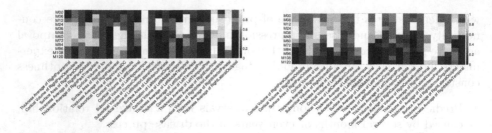

Fig. 2. Stability vectors of stable MRI features generated by STAC-L for cognitive tests using longitudinal stability selection. The left plot is conducted on MMSE dataset and the right plot on ADAS dataset.

TA of left temporal pole and TA of right lateral occipital shown a decreasing stability score by disease progression in ADAS-cog, while some features shown a high correlation in the middle stage, like CV of right pars opercularis, SV of right ventral DC and TA of right caudal middle frontal. The longitudinal stability selection shows a dynamical weighted stability scores ability of our method with heterogeneous scores of a vector in different stages of disease progression.

The identified biomarkers hippocampus and middle temporal as important central nodes in Fig. 2 have been found to predict AD progression [17,29]. The amygdala is affected early in AD and results from neuropsychiatric symptoms leading to functional deficits that greatly contribute to the disability associated with this disease [15]. In [26], researchers found widespread orbitofrontal damage including Parsorbitalis, transverse temporal and lateral orbitofrontal and this pathology may contribute heavily to the many non-memory-related behaviour changes observed in this disorder. [32] indicated a morphological change that only the precentral gyrus and superior parietal cortex were reduced in both left and right hemispheres. [12] demonstrated that the fusiform gyrus is critical in facial recognition and revealed the genetic and epigenetic basis of AD coupled with fusiform selected by our method as an important node in the biggest subset. Neuroanatomical studies in higher mammals reveal that the entorhinal cortex gives rise to axons that interconnect the hippocampal formation bidirectionally with the rest of the cortex [25].

All the above results have demonstrated that the proposed STAC model method not only yields superior performance on prediction accuracy, but is also a powerful tool for discovering structural imaging biomarkers related to AD progression. These results provide important information for understanding brain structural changes correlated with cognitive status and potentially help the characterization of AD progression.

4   Conclusions

In this article, we propose a new sparse multi-task learning model to correct the prior in both spatial and temporal relation learning. The proposed STAC model learns and exploits sparse structures related to disease progression based on Gaussian graphical model. Sparsity-inducing components achieved an adaptive scale constraint for both parameter sharing and accurate estimation of spatial feature connectivity. And a marginal distribution penalty helped in an adaptive correction of the deficiency for the existing longitudinal simulation method caused by ambiguous pathogenesis. In its application to the ADNI cohort, compared to multiple competing MTL progression models, STAC not only demonstrated superior prediction performance over them but also identified structural imaging biomarkers related to disease progression. The identified structural biomarkers are consistent with prior knowledge in existing literature. All the results have clearly demonstrated the effectiveness of STAC.

Acknowledgement. This research was supported by the National Natural Science Foundation of China (No. 62061050) and the 14th Postgraduate Research Innovation Project of Yunnan University (KC-22221162).

References

1. Beck, A., Teboulle, M.: A fast iterative shrinkage-thresholding algorithm for linear inverse problems. SIAM J. Imag. Sci. **2**(1), 183–202 (2009)
2. Boyd, S., Parikh, N., Chu, E., Peleato, B., Eckstein, J., et al.: Distributed optimization and statistical learning via the alternating direction method of multipliers. Found. Trends® Mach. Learn. **3**(1), 1–122 (2011)
3. Breijyeh, Z., Karaman, R.: Comprehensive review on Alzheimer's disease: causes and treatment. Molecules **25**(24), 5789 (2020)
4. Candes, E.J., Wakin, M.B., Boyd, S.P.: Enhancing sparsity by reweighted $\ell 1$ minimization. J. Fourier Anal. Appl. **14**, 877–905 (2008)
5. Caruana, R.: Multitask learning. Mach. Learn. **28**, 41–75 (1997)
6. Deng, Z., Yang, P., Zhao, Y., Zhao, X., Dong, F.: Life-logging data aggregation solution for interdisciplinary healthcare research and collaboration. In: 2015 IEEE International Conference on Computer and Information Technology; Ubiquitous Computing and Communications; Dependable, Autonomic and Secure Computing; Pervasive Intelligence and Computing, pp. 2315–2320. IEEE (2015)
7. Doraiswamy, P., Bieber, F., Kaiser, L., Krishnan, K., Reuning-Scherer, J., Gulanski, B.: The Alzheimer's disease assessment scale: patterns and predictors of baseline cognitive performance in multicenter alzheimer's disease trials. Neurology **48**(6), 1511–1517 (1997)
8. Gonçalves, A.R., Das, P., Chatterjee, S., Sivakumar, V., Von Zuben, F.J., Banerjee, A.: Multi-task sparse structure learning. In: Proceedings of the 23rd ACM International Conference on Conference on Information and Knowledge Management, pp. 451–460 (2014)
9. Huang, S., et al.: Learning brain connectivity of Alzheimer's disease from neuroimaging data. Adv. Neural Inf. Process. Syst. **22** (2009)
10. Li, Y., Liu, J., Tang, Z., Lei, B.: Deep spatial-temporal feature fusion from adaptive dynamic functional connectivity for MCI identification. IEEE Trans. Med. Imaging **39**(9), 2818–2830 (2020)
11. Liu, X., Cao, P., Gonçalves, A.R., Zhao, D., Banerjee, A.: Modeling Alzheimer's disease progression with fused Laplacian sparse group lasso. ACM Trans. Knowl. Discov. Data (TKDD) **12**(6), 1–35 (2018)

12. Ma, D., et al.: The fusiform gyrus exhibits an epigenetic signature for Alzheimer's disease. Clin. Epigenetics **12**(1), 1–16 (2020)
13. Nesterov, Y.: Introductory Lectures on Convex Optimization: A Basic Course, vol. 87. Springer, New York (2003). https://doi.org/10.1007/978-1-4419-8853-9
14. Parikh, N., Boyd, S., et al.: Proximal algorithms. Found. Trends® Optim. **1**(3), 127–239 (2014)
15. Poulin, S.P., Dautoff, R., Morris, J.C., Barrett, L.F., Dickerson, B.C., Initiative, A.D.N., et al.: Amygdala atrophy is prominent in early Alzheimer's disease and relates to symptom severity. Psychiatry Res. Neuroimaging **194**(1), 7–13 (2011)
16. Rai, P., Kumar, A., Daume, H.: Simultaneously leveraging output and task structures for multiple-output regression. Adv. Neural Inf. Process. Syst. **25** (2012)
17. Risacher, S.L., Saykin, A.J., Wes, J.D., Shen, L., Firpi, H.A., McDonald, B.C.: Baseline MRI predictors of conversion from MCI to probable AD in the ADNI cohort. Curr. Alzheimer Res. **6**(4), 347–361 (2009)
18. Robert, T.: Regression shrinkage and selection via the Lasso. J. Roy. Stat. Soc. B **58**, 267 (1994)
19. Rosen, W.G., Mohs, R.C., Davis, K.L.: A new rating scale for Alzheimer's disease. Am. J. Psychiatry **141**, 1356–1364 (1984)
20. Scheinberg, K., Ma, S., Goldfarb, D.: Sparse inverse covariance selection via alternating linearization methods. Adv. Neural Inf. Process. Syst. **23** (2010)
21. Spanakis, E.G., et al.: MyHealthAvatar: personalized and empowerment health services through internet of things technologies. In: 2014 4th International Conference on Wireless Mobile Communication and Healthcare-Transforming Healthcare Through Innovations in Mobile and Wireless Technologies (MOBIHEALTH), pp. 331–334. IEEE (2014)
22. Stonnington, C.M., et al.: Predicting clinical scores from magnetic resonance scans in Alzheimer's disease. Neuroimage **51**(4), 1405–1413 (2010)
23. Takahashi, T., Konishi, K., Furukawa, T.: Reweighted l 2 norm minimization approach to image inpainting based on rank minimization. In: 2011 IEEE 54th International Midwest Symposium on Circuits and Systems (MWSCAS), pp. 1–4. IEEE (2011)
24. Tierney, M.C., Nores, A., Snow, W.G., Fisher, R.H., Zorzitto, M.L., Reid, D.W.: Use of the Rey auditory verbal learning test in differentiating normal aging from Alzheimer's and Parkinson's dementia. Psychol. Assess. **6**(2), 129 (1994)
25. Van Hoesen, G.W., Hyman, B.T., Damasio, A.R.: Entorhinal cortex pathology in Alzheimer's disease. Hippocampus **1**(1), 1–8 (1991)
26. Van Hoesen, G.W., Parvizi, J., Chu, C.C.: Orbitofrontal cortex pathology in Alzheimer's disease. Cereb. Cortex **10**(3), 243–251 (2000)
27. Vandenberghe, L.: EE236C-optimization methods for large-scale systems. Lecture notes, 9 (2014)
28. Wan, J., et al.: Sparse Bayesian multi-task learning for predicting cognitive outcomes from neuroimaging measures in Alzheimer's disease. In: 2012 IEEE Conference on Computer Vision and Pattern Recognition, pp. 940–947. IEEE (2012)
29. Wang, L., et al.: Alterations in cortical thickness and white matter integrity in mild cognitive impairment measured by whole-brain cortical thickness mapping and diffusion tensor imaging. Am. J. Neuroradiol. **30**(5), 893–899 (2009)
30. Wang, X., Qi, J., Yang, Y., Yang, P.: A survey of disease progression modeling techniques for Alzheimer's diseases. In: 2019 IEEE 17th International Conference on Industrial Informatics (INDIN), vol. 1, pp. 1237–1242. IEEE (2019)
31. Weiner, M.W., et al.: The Alzheimer's disease neuroimaging initiative: progress report and future plans. Alzheimer's Dementia **6**(3), 202–211 (2010)

32. Yang, H., et al.: Study of brain morphology change in Alzheimer's disease and amnestic mild cognitive impairment compared with normal controls. General Psychiatry **32**(2) (2019)

33. Yang, J., Wang, S., Wu, T.: Maximum mutual information for feature extraction from graph-structured data: application to Alzheimer's disease classification. Appl. Intell. **53**(2), 1870–1886 (2023)

34. Yang, P., Yang, C., Lanfranchi, V., Ciravegna, F.: Activity graph based convolutional neural network for human activity recognition using acceleration and gyroscope data. IEEE Trans. Industr. Inf. **18**(10), 6619–6630 (2022)

35. Yang, P., et al.: DUAPM: an effective dynamic micro-blogging user activity prediction model towards cyber-physical-social systems. IEEE Trans. Industr. Inf. **16**(8), 5317–5326 (2019)

36. Zhang, Y., Lanfranchi, V., Wang, X., Zhou, M., Yang, P.: Modeling Alzheimer's disease progression via amalgamated magnitude-direction brain structure variation quantification and tensor multi-task learning. In: 2022 IEEE International Conference on Bioinformatics and Biomedicine (BIBM), pp. 2735–2742. IEEE (2022)

37. Zhang, Y., Yang, Q.: A survey on multi-task learning. IEEE Trans. Knowl. Data Eng. **34**(12), 5586–5609 (2021)

38. Zhou, J., Liu, J., Narayan, V.A., Ye, J., Initiative, A.D.N., et al.: Modeling disease progression via multi-task learning. Neuroimage **78**, 233–248 (2013)

39. Zhou, J., Yuan, L., Liu, J., Ye, J.: A multi-task learning formulation for predicting disease progression. In: Proceedings of the 17th ACM SIGKDD International Conference on Knowledge Discovery and Data Mining, pp. 814–822 (2011)

40. Zhou, M., Yang, P.: Automatic temporal relation in multi-task learning. In: Proceedings of the 29th ACM SIGKDD Conference on Knowledge Discovery and Data Mining, pp. 3570–3580 (2023)

41. Zhou, M., Zhang, Y., Yang, Y., Liu, T., Yang, P.: Robust temporal smoothness in multi-task learning. In: Proceedings of the AAAI Conference on Artificial Intelligence, vol. 37, pp. 11426–11434 (2023)

An Electromyographic Signal Acquisition System for Sarcopenia

Yihui Jian[1], Kaitai Mao[2], Jing Chen[3,4], Xinrui Ling[3], Ziguan Jin[1], Zhiqiu Ye[1], Geng Yang[1,5], Qin Zhang[3,4(✉)], and Kaichen Xu[1(✉)] (iD)

[1] State Key Laboratory of Fluid Power and Mechatronic Systems, School of Mechanical Engineering, Zhejiang University, Hangzhou 310000, China
xukc@zju.edu.cn
[2] School of Ocean Science and Engineering, Harbin Institute of Technology, Weihai, China
[3] Department of Geriatrics, First Affiliated Hospital, School of Medicine, Zhejiang University, Hangzhou, China
zhangqin1978@zju.edu.cn
[4] Key Laboratory of Diagnosis and Treatment of Aging and Physic-Chemical Injury Diseases of Zhejiang Province, School of Medicine, The First Affiliated Hospital, Zhejiang University, Hangzhou, Zhejiang, China
[5] Zhejiang Key Laboratory of Intelligent Operation and Maintenance Robot, Hangzhou, China

Abstract. Sarcopenia, characterized by age-related loss of strength and muscle mass, profoundly affects the elderly's well-being. Currently, diagnosing sarcopenia requires the utilization of extensive and cumbersome testing equipment. Surface electromyography (sEMG) is able to track muscle status and has been effectively employed in diagnosing various diseases or human-machine interactions, but its application in sarcopenia detection remains unexplored. In this study, a compact sEMG system is developed to monitor sarcopenia, which is endowed with compact dimensions, ease of operation, and wireless data transmission capabilities. The investigation involves the analysis of sEMG signals from 15 elderly participants. A significant correlation is established between the median frequency of these sEMG signals and the appendicular skeletal muscle mass (ASM). The proposed sEMG-based sarcopenia detection device exhibits the merit in portable use and highly operational efficiency. In future, it holds a high potential to replace the commercially cumbersome or non-portable testing devices, thereby facilitating widespread sarcopenia screening across diverse populations.

Keywords: Sarcopenia · sEMG · Wearable devices

1 Introduction

Sarcopenia is a newly defined disease in recent decades and has been paid great attentions. It is distinctly characterized by the age-related decline in skeletal muscle mass [1, 2], resulting in sluggish mobility and reduced strength among the elderly. Notably, it leads to muscle convulsions, spasms, falls, fractures, and other related complications [3, 4]. The influence of sarcopenia on human's health is profound, greatly compromising the living

J. Qi and P. Yang (Eds.): IoTBDH 2023, CCIS 2019, pp. 84–93, 2024.
https://doi.org/10.1007/978-3-031-52216-1_7

quality of middle-aged and elderly people. More seriously, it can threaten their lives [5]. Fortunately, there are currently good nutritional interventions and exercise methods for sarcopenia to alleviate its deterioration. Therefore, a timely diagnosis of sarcopenia is necessary.

Currently, the diagnosis of sarcopenia needs a comprehensive evaluation including three key factors: muscle strength, physical performance, and ASM [6]. Muscle strength and physical performance can be measured simply by grip strength and gait speed, respectively. However, ASM requires the help of large instruments. The current optimal option to measure muscle mass relies on utilizing Dual-energy X-ray absorptiometry (DEXA), which is capable of precisely quantifying ASM. Limited by the high cost, bulky, and radiation, it is mainly used in the larger medical facilities. A suitable alternative to quantify the ASM is bioelectrical impedance analysis (BIA) [7], which offers greater user-friendliness. Nonetheless, fluctuations in cellular impedance that are highly related to body conditions greatly influence the test's accuracy, especially when the body suffers from dehydration or edema. Although lower cost is available for the BIA equipment, it is still not affordable for some community hospitals or individuals. Hence, it is of vital significance to design a simple, convenient, and economical ASM assessment tool for extensive sarcopenia screening [8, 9].

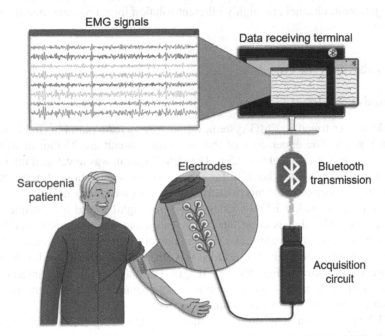

Fig. 1 An sEMG signal acquisition system for sarcopenia. It is composed of acquisition electrodes, an sEMG signal processing system, a mobile user interface with Bluetooth for wireless data transmission, and an sEMG-based sarcopenia analysis system

One promising approach is the use of sEMG to diagnose sarcopenia. It serves as a modality and technique capable of providing an objective representation of the bioelectrical activity within the neuromuscular system [10]. It shows the unique advantages of easy operation, non-invasive and multi-faceted target detection [11, 12]. The sEMG signals contain a wealth of information that reflect the muscle activities for effective diagnosis of sarcopenia. Until now, although a few investigations on sEMG signals have been conducted to diagnose various diseases like Parkinson's disease, cerebral palsy in children, and spinal cord injuries [13], a pragmatic and effective diagnostic approach for sarcopenia is still under exploration.

Here, an sEMG signal acquisition system tailored for sarcopenia detection has been proposed (Fig. 1). This system allows for the efficient acquisition of eight-channel sEMG signals and enables a comparable performance to commercial sEMG electrodes. Notably, it is equipped with a low-power Bluetooth module for wireless data transmission. Owing to its user-friendly operation and reliable performance, we established collaborations with a local hospital (The First Affiliated Hospital, Zhejiang University School of Medicine). This collaboration includes a data acquisition task of sEMG signals from 15 elderly participants. Subsequently, relevant feature signals have been extracted from these sEMG signals to reveal certain eigenvalues corresponding to muscle mass measurements obtained via BIA. Our proposed sEMG detection system offers a low cost, lightweight, multi-channel and highly efficient solution for sarcopenia identification in the future.

2   Acquisition System

2.1   Acquisition Circuit

To enable an user-friendly sEMG system, we have designed a portable circuit, as illustrated in Fig. 2A. The dimensions of the acquisition circuit are 23 mm in width and 56 mm in length, with a weight of 7.5 g. The sEMG system was developed not only for portable testing in hospitals, but also for some wearable applications. Importantly, the lightweight of this circuit also meets the requirement of wearing comforts.

Obtaining high-quality EMG signals is not a straightforward task, primarily due to the fact that EMG signals constitute a type of minute signal characterized by high source impedance. Consequently, we have iteratively refined and optimized the data acquisition system multiple times to address this challenge. The hardware block diagram of the circuit is depicted in Fig. 2B. This diagram displays two primary interfaces that connected with the external environment: an eight-channel EMG input interface and a Bluetooth wireless data transmission interface.

For EMG input and acquisition, an integrated ADC chip (ADS1198) was used. Although the conventional approach involves employing discrete components to filter and amplify the EMG signals, subsequently utilizing the ADC of MCU for signal collection, two primary challenges still exist:

1) Increased PCB board area: The use of discrete devices results in an expanded PCB board area, which hampers the pursuit of miniaturization and integration.

2) ADC accuracy limitation: The Successive Approximation Register (SAR) ADC fea-
tured in the MCU entails limited accuracy, rendering it suboptimal for our needs.
By utilizing ADS1198 physiological electrical signal acquisition chip, circuit miniaturization, acquisition accuracy, and isolation of superior analog from digital signal
during the PCB layout process can be achieved. This is a critical step in achieving a
portable and lightweight sEMG system.

For data transmission, the transceiver functionality can be obtained by using a chip
(STM32WB55CGU6) equipped with Bluetooth function. By leveraging this MCU, we
obviate the need for a standalone Bluetooth chip, leading to a substantial reduction in the
acquisition circuit's dimensions. Moreover, the inclusion of built-in Bluetooth module
of the MCU fosters enhance efficiency in data exchange between the central processing
unit and the Bluetooth stack. This synergy translates to a more judicious utilization of
Bluetooth communication bandwidth, thereby enhancing overall performance.

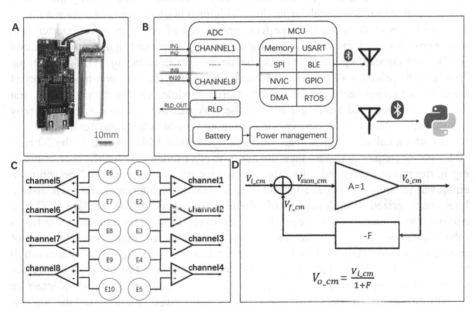

Fig. 2 Illustrates of the electromyographic signal acquisition system. (A) Physical diagram of the
sEMG signal acquisition circuitry. (B) Schematic representation of the sEMG signal acquisition
system, including the functions of signal collection, data packaging, and wireless transmission via
Bluetooth to the user-end receiver. (C) Depiction of the attachment of electromyographic electrodes, wherein the positive and negative inputs of two adjacent channels are connected, necessitating the affixation of a total of ten electrodes for the eight-channel electromyographic signal.
(D) Signal diagram of the right-foot driving module, employed for common-mode interference
suppression

2.2 Electrode Attachment

The proposed electromyographic signal detection equipment facilitates the concurrent collection of 8 channels of electromyographic signals. During the detection process, electrodes are affixed to two columns along the muscle fibers, as illustrated in Fig. 2C. The EMG signal is acquired using a differential method, necessitating the use of two electrodes per channel. The positive input and negative input of adjacent channels are linked. This configuration significantly reduces the electrode count, thereby fostering a more concentrated channel arrangement. Each column accommodates a total of four channels, leading to deploy five electrodes per column, with the two adjacent electrodes jointly forming a channel.

Given the substantial impedance of human skin, the acquisition of EMG signals is susceptible to be interfered by common-mode voltage. To counteract this, we have incorporated a reference electrode to achieve voltage balance. This reference electrode is positioned on an area of human skin devoid of muscle tissue. During the testing phase, we observed that merely grounding the human body in synchronization with the acquisition device does not yield perfect suppression of common-mode interference. In response, we drew inspiration from the commonly employed right foot drive circuit (RLD) in electrocardiogram (ECG) acquisition, as illustrated in Fig. 2D. This tecnique leverages the principle of negative feedback, channeling the common-mode aspect of the collected signal back into the right foot drive module. This approach ensures that the reference potential along the entire collection pathway remains at zero, thereby significantly enhancing the suppression of common-mode voltage interference.

An additional interference that considerably impacts EMG signals is the 50 Hz / 60 Hz power frequency disturbance, arising from electromagnetic interference originating in the power mains and infiltrating the acquisition circuit as noise. The approach employed to address this issue involves the utilization of interfaces and transmission lines characterized by high degrees of shielding effectiveness. The standard ECG lead equipped with ten collection electrodes is employed. This choice hinges on the lead's robust shielding layer, which serves to curtail the ingress of interference. In terms of interfaces, our preference is the HDMI interface lead. In contrast to the traditional DB19 interface, the HDMI interface has a more compact form fact. For the RLD drive electrode, we have implemented a shielded lead wire for connection. The MMCX interface is skillfully integrated, welding it to establish a link between the lead and the acquisition circuit. MMCX interface is commonly employed for transmitting audio signals in earphones, showcasing compact physical dimensions with exemplary signal shielding capabilities.

3 Data Collection

Upon finalizing the design of acquisition system, we start formulating the data collection strategy. Our primary objective includes the EMG data collection from elderly individuals afflicted with sarcopenia, juxtaposed with EMG data collection from a reference group of normal elderly individuals.

Following comprehensive analysis and rigorous testing, the bicep muscle emerged as the chosen test muscle. This selection was grounded in several pivotal factors: 1)

The bicep muscle's attachment area was devoid of other muscles, ensuring that the collection process remained unaffected by interference from neighboring muscles. 2) The bicep muscle's force action was relatively straightforward and easily quantifiable, rendering it amenable to testing. While leg muscles are often preferred for sarcopenia [14, 15], we recognized that leg EMG signals present a testing challenge, unlike the biceps. Consequently, we made a deliberate decision to focus on the bicep muscle to facilitate targeted data collection.

During the experimental phase, we incorporated two distinct actions as our testing protocols: the Muscle Maximal Voluntary Contraction (MVC) and a Fixed Tension Test using a weight of 2 kg. As depicted in Fig. 3A, it was essential for participants to maintain vertical alignment of their forearms and upper arms throughout the testing. The MVC test served the purpose of standardizing the amplitude of EMG. The 2 kg fixed tension test required participants to sustain the posture illustrated in Fig. 3B for a duration of 2 m. Throughout this period, continuous EMG signal data were recorded. Thus, each participant yielded a set of both MVC signals and fixed tension test signals.

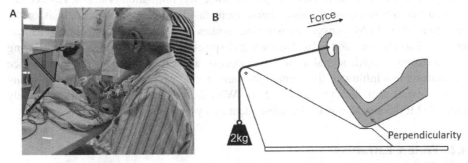

Fig. 3 Electromyographic signal acquisition schematic. (A) Photograph taken during the electromyographic signal collection at the hospital, illustrating electrodes attached to the biceps brachii, wherein the participant's muscle contraction is employed to lift a weight. (B) Illustrative diagram of the testing setup, requiring the forearm to be perpendicular to the upper arm

In the preliminary testing phase, we also explored incorporating repetitive dumbbell lifts as a testing action. However, due to challenges related to the cognitive capabilities of elderly participants, many struggled to complete the exercise test according to the stipulated standards. Consequently, we opted not to include this action in our final testing regime.

The corresponding EMG signals acquisition from participants have been approved by ethical committees of the 1st affiliated hospital of Zhejiang University. The related electrodes placement on human participants and the collection of EMG signals were conducted by professional medical staffs. We finally left 15 participants, eight of whom were diagnosed with sarcopenia, while others represented healthy individuals.

4 Data Analysis

4.1 Preconditioning

The original EMG signals inherently exhibit baseline drift and are susceptible to noise interference. The extraction of accurate, stable, and dependable information from the original EMG signal necessitates the elimination of these sources of interference, thereby facilitating subsequent analysis. The initial step is to eliminate baseline drift from the electromyographic signals. Both the moving average and wavelet transform techniques are capable of extracting baseline components from the EMG signals. By subtracting the baseline-extracted EMG signal from the original, an EMG signal devoid of baseline drift can be obtained. However, we opted for a simpler strategy: high-pass Butterworth filter.

Given that EMG signals primarily occupy the frequency range of 6 to 400 Hz, with the majority of energy concentrated between 20 and 150 Hz [16], the utilization of a 6–400 Hz bandpass Butterworth filter effectively removes extraneous components. Recognizing baseline drift as low-frequency noise, its elimination is seamlessly accomplished through bandpass filtering. Subsequent fast Fourier transform analysis of the bandpass-filtered EMG unveils conspicuous spikes corresponding to 50 Hz and its harmonics. This phenomenon led to deduce that despite the incorporation of shielding during the electromyographic signal acquisition process, a fraction of power-line interference has nonetheless infiltrated the signal. To counter this, we implemented notch filtering at frequencies such as 50 Hz and 150 Hz. With these steps, we arrived at a relatively untainted EMG signal, poised for subsequent analysis.

4.2 Feature Extraction

The gamut of features extractable from EMG encompasses time domain features, frequency domain features, and nonlinear features. When delving into time domain features, the utilization of MVC test outcomes is indispensable to normalize EMG amplitude obtained during sustained tension tests. This corrective action is mandated by the variations in individuals' skin thickness and adipose tissue content, which significantly influence EMG amplitude. The exploration of frequency domain indices requires the Fourier transform of the EMG signal. Nonlinear features have emerged as electromyographic signal analysis features in recent years. They have demonstrated significant efficacy in the domain of muscle fatigue assessment [17]. Consequently, we have also harnessed the potential of fractal dimension features extracted from the EMG for analysis endeavors. Specifically, the box dimension algorithm is employed to calculate fractal dimension values. In sum, we extracted fractal dimension (FD), median frequency (MF), root mean square (RMS), variance (VAR), kurtosis (KUR), and peak-factor (PF) from the EMG signal. In the hospital-based assessments, we additionally employed BIA to evaluate participants' ASM. Comprehensive results are displayed in Table 1.

Table 1. The clinical indices and electromyographic characteristics of each participant

ID	Age	Type	ASM	FD	MF	RMS	VAR	KUR	PF
1	85	S	3.93	1.59	103.85	0.119	0.0152	4.16	4.19
2	83	H	8.07	1.58	84.90	0.075	0.0057	3.41	3.75
3	88	H	6.91	1.58	81.04	0.146	0.0220	3.38	3.74
4	89	S	5.6	1.59	90.70	0.080	0.0066	3.38	3.75
5	86	S	3.41	1.58	115.47	0.066	0.0053	5.07	4.56
6	81	H	5.81	1.58	85.85	0.084	0.0078	3.46	3.84
7	91	S	3.39	1.60	114.00	0.091	0.0092	3.99	4.15
8	94	S	5.51	1.59	115.18	0.244	0.0630	4.64	4.43
9	92	H	6.77	1.59	95.90	0.085	0.0081	3.47	3.83
10	72	S	4.94	1.60	104.99	0.100	0.0118	3.59	3.90
11	83	S	5.34	1.59	91.07	0.090	0.0082	3.32	3.71
12	93	S	4.5	1.59	100.28	0.163	0.0290	3.64	3.94
13	94	H	5.89	1.60	98.72	0.174	0.0315	3.47	3.84
14	90	H	7.81	1.57	83.05	0.121	0.0151	3.55	3.88
15	87	H	5.72	1.59	85.70	0.053	0.0034	3.30	3.61

[*] S = Sarcopenia; H = Healthy People

4.3 Results

While deep learning and machine learning have gained wide attentions in EMG signal analysis, particularly in the realm of motion recognition [18, 19], their reception in the medical domain remains relatively reserved. On the other hand, traditional mathematical and statistical methodologies are often preferred due to their higher degree of comprehensibility. Such approaches allow medical professionals to gain a clearer understanding of how a model reaches conclusions, enhancing applicability in clinical practice. Thus, when analyzing the relationship between electromyography and sarcopenia, we adopt mathematical techniques for feature extraction and employed statistical methods to investigate correlations between electromyography features and established clinical features.

The analysis encompassed the correlation between the six features derived from the EMG signal and ASM from BIA. Eventually, a good linear correlation between the median frequency and body composition is achieved (Fig. 4). This correlation shows a coefficient of 0.774 with a significant p-value of 0.001.

The calculation process of MF is relatively straightforward. It involves transforming a time-domain signal within a time window into a frequency-domain signal using Fourier transformation. The frequency at which the power on both sides of the spectrum is equal is defined as the median frequency. Fortunately, the efficiency of calculation is significantly improved by the FFT (Fast Fourier Transform). In the future, there is potential for the integration of this algorithm within the data acquisition system, enabling offline analysis

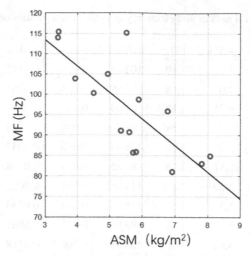

Fig. 4 Relationship between electromyographic median frequency and appendicular skeletal muscle mass (ASM), correlation = 0.774, p < 0.001, N = 15

of sarcopenia. The utilization of median frequency analysis of ASM has the potential to substantially streamline the detection process and reduce testing costs.

5 Conclusion

To address the challenges encountered in sarcopenia diagnosis, particularly the expensive and non-portable nature of ASM testing equipment, an electromyographic signal acquisition system is developed for sarcopenia assessment. This innovative system enables eight-channel sampling at a high 2 kHz rate, with real-time transmission to a personal computer via Bluetooth. Leveraging this technology, EMG signals are successfully collected from 15 elderly women with the extraction of six distinct characteristic values. Notably, the median frequency exhibits a robust correlation with body composition. The electromyography feature obtained through this testing methodology holds the potential as an alternative benchmark for body composition assessment towards future clinical standards.

Beyond its diagnostic applications, this collection system has the potential to transition into a community-level device for large-scale sarcopenia screening. Its deployment can significantly contribute to early sarcopenia diagnosis, extending the benefits of timely intervention to a broader demographic.

References

1. Rosenberg, I.H.: Sarcopenia: origins and clinical relevance. J. Nutr. **127**(5), 990S–991S (1997)
2. Boirie, Y.: Physiopathological mechanism of sarcopenia. JNHA - J. Nutr. Health Aging **13**(8), 717–723 (2009)

3. Landi, F., et al.: Sarcopenia as a risk factor for falls in elderly individuals: results from the ilSIRENTE study. Clin. Nutr. **31**(5), 652–658 (2012)
4. Tarantino, U., et al.: Osteoporosis and sarcopenia: the connections. Aging Clin. Exp. Res. **25**, 93–95 (2013)
5. Landi, F., et al.: Sarcopenia and mortality risk in frail older persons aged 80 years and older: results from ilSIRENTE study. Age Ageing **42**(2), 203–209 (2013)
6. Chen, L.-K., et al.: Asian working group for sarcopenia: 2019 consensus update on sarcopenia diagnosis and treatment. J. Am. Med. Directors Assoc. **21**(3), 300–307.e2 (2020)
7. Cruz-Jentoft, A.J., et al.: Sarcopenia: revised European consensus on definition and diagnosis. Age Ageing **48**(1), 16–31 (2019)
8. Sergi, G., De Rui, M., Stubbs, B., Veronese, N., Manzato, E.: Measurement of lean body mass using bioelectrical impedance analysis: a consideration of the pros and cons. Aging Clin. Exp. Res. **29**, 591–597 (2017)
9. Hioka, A., Akazawa, N., Okawa, N., Nagahiro, S.: Extracellular water-to-total body water ratio is an essential confounding factor in bioelectrical impedance analysis for sarcopenia diagnosis in women. Eur. Geriatr. Med. **13**(4), 789–794 (2022)
10. Norali, A.N., Som, M., Kangar-Arau, J.: Surface electromyography signal processing and application: a review. In: Proceedings of the International Conference on Man-Machine Systems (ICoMMS), no. 11–13 (2009)
11. Garcia, M.C., Vieira, T.M.M.: Surface electromyography: why, when and how to use it. Revista andaluza de medicina del deporte **4**(1), 17–28 (2011)
12. Reaz, M.B.I., Hussain, M.S., Mohd-Yasin, F.: Techniques of EMG signal analysis: detection, processing, classification and applications. Biological Proced. Online **8**, 11–35 (2006)
13. Balbinot, G., Li, G., Wiest, M.J., Pakosh, M., Furlan, J.C., Kalsi-Ryan, S., Zariffa, J.: Properties of the surface electromyogram following traumatic spinal cord injury: a scoping review. J. NeuroEngineering Rehabil. **18**(1), 105 (2021)
14. Fialkoff, B., et al.: Hand grip force estimation via EMG imaging. Biomed. Signal Process. Control **74**, 103550 (2022)
15. Chen, I., et al.: Sarcopenia recognition system combined with electromyography and gait obtained by the multiple sensor module and deep learning algorithm. Sens. Mater. **34**(6), 2403 (2022)
16. Webster, J.: Medical Instrumentation: Application and Design, Wiley (2010)
17. Rampichini, S., et al.: Complexity analysis of surface electromyography for assessing the myoelectric manifestation of muscle fatigue: a review. Entropy **22**(5), 529 (2020)
18. Moin, A., et al.: A wearable biosensing system with in-sensor adaptive machine learning for hand gesture recognition. Nat. Electron. **4**(1), 54–63 (2021)
19. Tang, W., et al.: Delamination-resistant imperceptible bioelectrode for robust electrophysiological signals monitoring. ACS Mater. Lett. **3**(9), 1385–1393 (2021)

Machine Learning-Based Metabolic Syndrome Identification

Chang Liu[1]([⊠])[iD], Jingjing Liu[1][iD], Zhangdaihong Liu[2][iD], and Yang Yang[1][iD]

[1] Shanghai Jiao Tong University, Shanghai 200025, China
{nt-liuchang2018,liujingjing123123,emma002}@sjtu.edu.cn
[2] Oxford Suzhou Center For Adcanced Research, Suzhou 215123, Jiangsu, China
Jessie.Liu@oxford-oscar.cn

Abstract. Objective: To explore the efficacy of machine learning techniques in identifying Metabolic Syndrome (MetS) and examine the performance of models when applied to target populations with different distributions. **Methods**: This study utilizes data from the National Health and Nutrition Examination Survey (NHANES) and local physical examinations, where MetS is diagnosed based on the International Diabetes Federation (IDF) standards. We first employ demographic and blood test data from NHANES and predicted MetS using machine learning models (including MLP, Logistic Regression, Random Forest, XGBoost, Catboost, and Multi-layer Perceptron), and then test these predictions on different population data. **Results**: Models employing 59 features demonstrate commendable performance in the NHANES test set (same population testing), with the MLP model exhibiting the best performance (AUROC= 0.93). Models constructed with 32 features (excluding height, weight, and certain blood test information) still show promising results (MLP AUROC = 0.89). However, when the models are tested on the local physical examination dataset (cross-population testing), there is a substantial decline in performance (MLP AUROC = 0.71). **Conclusion**: Machine learning techniques can predict MetS on the NHANES dataset with high accuracy. Due to the distribution shift, examined machine learning models perform better in the setting with same population distribution.

Keywords: Metabolic Syndrome · Machine Learning · Population Health Management

1 Introduction

Metabolic syndrome (MetS) is an early subclinical syndrome characterized by the aggregation of multiple risk factors of metabolic diseases. The main indicators of MetS include abdominal obesity, elevated blood pressure, hyperglycemia, hyperlipidemia, and low high-density lipoprotein cholesterol. Existing researches have shown that MetS is closely associated with the risk of numerous chronic non-communicable diseases, such as coronary heart diseases, stroke, diabetes,

© The Author(s), under exclusive license to Springer Nature Switzerland AG 2024
J. Qi and P. Yang (Eds.): IoTBDH 2023, CCIS 2019, pp. 94–101, 2024.
https://doi.org/10.1007/978-3-031-52216-1_8

and hypertension [1]. As a result, it has become a significant disease burden in the field of public health and a focal issue in recent population health management (PHM) [2,3].

Machine learning (ML) technology has been increasingly utilized in clinical areas [4]. The timely and accurately detection and diagnosis of diseases through machine learning remains a consistent and prominent topic in scientific research. Concurrently, the widespread application of AI technology has fostered the rapid growth of PHM, which aims to enable all individuals within a specific population to maintain and enhance their health. With the evolution and implementation of advanced machine learning models, population health research can model multidimensional health data from large cohorts to extract valuable insights, further applying these findings to PHM [5].

The diagnosis of metabolic syndrome (MetS), according to the diagnostic criteria in the joint statement by the International Diabetes Federation (IDF), involves multiple physical meOSasurements and laboratory tests, such as waist circumference, blood pressure, blood sugar, triglycerides, and high-density lipoprotein cholesterol, which obviously presents certain limitations in the context of PHM or individual health management. Among the others, waist circumference is the indicator that is fairly stable and can be conveniently measured. The blood pressure and blood sugar require multiple measures to confirm the reliability. The triglycerides, and high-density lipoprotein cholesterol need to be tested in hospital with lab analyser. The gold standards for the blood sugar, riglycerides, and high-density lipoprotein cholesterol are tested intrusively. In this case, out-of-hospital diagnosis of MetS has become challenging, thus, the exploiting of other valuable indicators and the use of ML approaches to assist the remote monitoring and detection in the early stage is immensely valuable.

In clinical scenarios, if a patient is suspected to have MetS, endocrinologists will be involved in the diagnosis and treatment pipeline. Patients will receive advice from endocrinologists on lifestyle management. However, this process can be time-consuming and labor-intensive, and there is also a certain risk of missed or misdiagnosis.

Given these challenges, this research aims achieve early identification of MetS using ML technologies with population health data. Better classification of MetS will assist the timely detection of MetS and thus improve personal health management.

2   Datasets and Methods

2.1   Datasets

Data Sources. In this study, we utilized the public database from the National Health and Nutrition Examination Survey (NHANES), which is a national survey program conducted by the U.S. National Center for Health Statistics. Initiated in 1960, this program periodically evaluates the health and nutritional status of the American population, collecting relevant clinical, demographic, and nutritional data. NHANES stands as one of the largest ongoing health surveys in the US population, offering a comprehensive dataset on population health, which can be employed to research various health issues, such as MetS, diabetes, and cardiovascular diseases. The NHANES survey adopts multistage sampling techniques, including random sampling, stratified sampling, and cluster sampling. Participants undergo questionnaire interviews, physical examinations, and biological sample collections. The comprehensive NHANES dataset encompasses numerous physiological indicators, biochemical markers, nutritional indices, disease diagnoses, medication usage, and health behaviors [6,7].

We used the NHANES data from 1999–2018, encompassing 101,316 individuals, and a local health examination dataset, encompassing 10,446 individuals, forming the original datasets for this study.

Diagnosis of Metabolic Syndrome. In this study, we diagnosed MetS based on the standards and definitions set forth in the joint statement by the IDF [8]. According to this criterion, MetS is diagnosed when three or more of the following five components are present:

1) Increased waist circumference ($\geq$88cm for females, $\geq$102cm for males);
2) Elevated triglycerides (TG) ($\geq$150mg/dL) or currently undergoing treatment for hyperlipidemia;
3) Reduced high-density lipoprotein cholesterol (HDL-c) (<40mg/dL for males, <50mg/dL for females) or currently undergoing treatment for low HDL-c;
4) Elevated blood pressure (systolic blood pressure (SBP) $\geq$130mmHg or diastolic blood pressure (DBP) $\geq$85mmHg or both) or currently on antihypertensive treatment or with a history of hypertension;
5) Elevated fasting blood glucose (FBG) ($\geq$100mg/dL) or currently undergoing treatment for hyperglycemia.

Using the questionnaire information and biochemical data of participants provided by NHANES, such as blood glucose, triglycerides, and HDL-C, we diagnosed each component [9]. NHANES did not collect laboratory test information for HDL-C during the survey years from 1999 to 2004. Thus, we substituted this with medication treatment information reported in the questionnaire. Ultimately, 55,684 participants with sufficient information were diagnosed, of which 19,530 (35.1%) were categorized as MetS.

Features. As is a specialized, large-scale cross-sectional study, NHANES data encompasses various features ranging from demographic, anthropometric, to blood test variables. Given the distinct feature sets in NHANES and local health examination datasets, we utilized the overlapping feature subset in this study. We primarily based our choices on the features available in the local health examination dataset. Firstly, after excluding indicators for MetS diagnosis, we identified common demographic, anthropometric, and blood test features present in both the local health examination dataset and the NHANES dataset (a total of 59 features). Due to the issue of missing data in the local physical examination dataset, we ultimately established two feature settings encompassing 59 features and 32 features respectively, and three different experiments (Table 1). Specifically, Experiment 1 involved modeling using 59 variables in the NHANES dataset and testing in an independent validation set selected from the NHANES population. Experiments 2 and 3 utilized the same NHANES training data, with an input of 32 features, and were tested on the independent validation set from NHANES and the local dataset, respectively. Table 2 illustrates the full names and corresponding abbreviations of the features.

Table 1. Features included in different experiments

Experiment	Features
1	sex, age, BUN, UA, TBIL, TP, Glo, Alb, Cr, ALT, AST, TC, NENO, NEPCT, MOPCT, MONO, BANO, BAPCT, EONO, EOPCT, MPV, MCHC, MCH, LY, LYPCT, WBC, RBC, RDW_CV, HCT, MCV, PLT, Hb, GGT, ALP, Sodium, kalium, CRP, Insulin, Lead, LDH, HbA1c, Height, Weight, LDL, HAV, HBsAg, HBcAb, HCV, HBsAb
2	sex, age, BUN, UA, TBIL, TP, Glo, Alb, Cr, ALT, AST, TC, NENO, NEPCT, MOPCT, MONO, BANO, BAPCT, EONO, EOPCT, MPV, MCHC, MCH, LY, LYPCT, WBC, RBC, RDW_CV, HCT, MCV, PLT, Hb
3	sex, age, BUN, UA, TBIL, TP, Glo, Alb, Cr, ALT, AST, TC, NENO, NEPCT, MOPCT, MONO, BANO, BAPCT, EONO, EOPCT, MPV, MCHC, MCH, LY, LYPCT, WBC, RBC, RDW_CV, HCT, MCV, PLT, Hb

2.2 Methods

Data Preprocessing. The preprocessing of the data commenced with the identification of outliers in each column, those values falling outside the range ($<$Q1-$1.5\times$IQR, $>$Q3+$1.5\times$IQR) were regarded as outliers. Adopting a stratified approach based on varied age and gender demographics, any missing value in each feature was substituted with the mean value of that particular feature derived from specific age-gender subgroup. For categorical variables, missing values were imputed with a distinct value and subsequently transformed into dummy variables.

The NHANES dataset was splitted into a training set (38,978 samples) and a test set (16,706 samples) randomly with the "train_test_split" function in the "scikit-learn" package, while the whole local dataset was employed as an independent validation test set (10,446 samples). Subsequently, using the "QuantileTransformer" function in the "scikit-learn" package (Python, version 0.23.2)

Table 2. Abbreviation of the features included

Feature names	Abbreviation
Gender	sex
Age	age
Triglycerides	TG
Fasting blood glucose	FBG
Systolic blood pressure	SBP
Diastolic blood pressure	DBP
Blood urea nitrogen	BUN
Urine acid	UA
Total bilirubin	TBIL
Total protein	TP
Globulin	Glo
Albumin	Alb
Creatinine	Cr
Alanine transaminase	ALT
Aspartate transaminase	AST
Total cholesterol	TC
Neutrocyte number	NENO
Neutrocyte percentage	NEPCT
Monocytes percentage	MOPCT
Monocytes number	MONO
Basophils number	BANO
Basophils percentage	BAPCT
Eosinophils number	EONO
Eosinophils number	EOPCT
Mean platelet volume	MPV
Mean corpuscular hemoglobin concentration	MCHC
Mean corpuscular hemoglobin content	MCH
Lymphocytes number	LY
Lymphocytes percentage	LYPCT
White blood cell count	WBC
Red blood cell count	RBC
Coefficient of variation of red blood cell distribution width	RDW_CV
Hematocrit	HCT
Mean corpuscular volume	MCV
Platelet	PLT
Hemoglobin	Hb
Gamma-Glutamyl Transpeptidase	GGT
Alkaline Phosphatase	ALP
Sodium	Sodium
Kalium	kalium
C-reactive Protein	CRP
Insulin	Insulin
Lead	Lead
Lactate Dehydrogenase	LDH
Hemoglobin A1c	HbA1c
Height	Height
Weight	Weight
Low Density Lipoprotein	LDL
Hepatitis A Virus	HAV
Hepatitis B Surface Antigen	HBsAg
Hepatitis B Core Antibody	HBcAb
Hepatitis C Virus	HCV
Hepatitis B Surface Antibody	HBsAb

to normalise the datasets. This non-linear and independent transformation technique converts raw values into uniform distribution values sampled from the estimated cumulative distribution function of the feature. To mitigate the potential adverse effects of sample imbalance on training efficacy, the Synthetic Minority Over-sampling Technique (SMOTE) was used to oversample the MetS positive population within the training set. Table 3 presents the sample size for each dataset.

Table 3. Size of datasets

Datasets	Sample size
NHANES training set	38,978
NHANES testing set	16,706
Local Dataset	10,446

Models. We employed various machine learning models including Logistic Regression (LR), Random Forest (RF), XGBoost, Catboost, as well as the Multilayer Perceptron (MLP). We used 10-fold cross-validation and optimised each model, subsequently training the models with these optimal settings [10]. For the MLP model, the hyper-parameters and model architectures were optimised by a random search, with the model then being trained using this configuration.

Evaluation. Accuracy, Precision, Recall, F1-score, and the Area Under the ROC curve (AUROC) are used to evaluating the performance of the models. Accuracy measures the proportion of samples correctly classified out of the total, representing the model's ability to classify correctly. Precision indicates the proportion of positive predictions that were actually positive, reflecting the precision of the model's classification. Recall represents the proportion of actual positive samples that the model correctly predicted as positive, indicating the model's coverage of positive samples. The F1-score is the harmonic mean of Precision and Recall, serving as an integrated metric to assess the classification performance of the model. AUROC, determined by calculating the area under the ROC curve, depicts the relationship between the true positive rate and the false positive rate across different thresholds, revealing the classifier's performance under various thresholds.

3   Results

Firstly, we trained models using 59 features and 32 features respectively in the NHANES dataset and evaluated the models on a unified hold-out test set.

As shown in Table 4, all five models achieved satisfactory results, with nearly all evaluation metrics exceeding 0.8. Among all five models, the MLP demonstrated the best performance, achieving top-tier results in every performance

Table 4. Performance of the models in the NHANES dataset

Experiment	Models	Accuracy	Precision	Recall	F1	AUROC	AUPRC
1	LR	0.847	**0.744**	0.865	0.800	0.851	0.828
	RF	0.835	0.718	0.877	0.790	0.845	0.819
	XGBoost	0.839	0.729	0.867	0.792	0.845	0.822
	Catboost	0.777	0.618	**0.968**	0.754	0.820	0.799
	MLP	**0.848**	0.739	0.879	**0.803**	**0.929**	**0.858**
2	LR	**0.810**	**0.692**	0.832	0.755	0.815	**0.791**
	RF	0.803	0.673	0.858	0.754	0.815	**0.791**
	XGBoost	0.784	0.636	0.903	0.747	0.811	0.787
	Catboost	0.718	0.559	**0.962**	0.707	0.774	0.767
	MLP	0.806	0.680	0.855	**0.758**	**0.894**	0.782

evaluation metric. The LR shows the best in precision. The nonlinear ensemble models like XGBoost and Catboost, although they had high Recall values, performed worse than MLP and LR.

Additionally, when comparing the results of models with 59 features against those with 32 features in NHANES only, it is evident that, although there was a decline in performance across all models, the magnitude of this decline wasn't significant. This implies that after eliminating body measurements like height, weight, and additional blood test features, the models were not significantly affected.

By evaluate the performance of the models trained on NHANES when applied to different populations of local dataset (with 32 features), as shown in Table 5, it indicated that the MLP still outperformed the others. Overall, compared to their counterpart on the NHANES dataset, all the models witnessed a substantial decline in performance. For instance, the AUROC score of the best-performing model, MLP, dropped from 0.89 to 0.71.

Table 5. Performance of the models in the local dataset

Models	Accuracy	Precision	Recall	F1	AUROC	AUPRC
LR	**0.671**	**0.381**	0.621	0.472	0.654	0.546
RF	0.623	0.350	0.682	0.462	0.644	0.554
XGBoost	0.634	0.356	0.668	0.464	0.646	0.551
Catboost	0.441	0.286	**0.906**	0.435	0.601	**0.607**
MLP	0.661	0.375	0.645	**0.475**	**0.710**	0.423

4   Discussion

In our experiments, we explored a variety of machine learning models for MetS classification based on demographic and blood test indicators. Through multiple model and dataset configurations, we discerned that the MLP model showed superior performance in this context. It is noted that the inclusion or exclusion of variables like height and weight, which are conventionally strongly associated with MetS, did not have a significant impact on model performance. Most crucially, our experiment exhibited considerable variability in model performance when applied across different populations. This underscores a potential distribution shift across various regions and demographic characteristics. Hence, transferring a model to be applied to a different population distribution necessitates a judicious approach. Enhancing the model's generalization capability through continual learning strategies remains a future objective of this study.

References

1. Grundy, S.M., et al.: Diagnosis and management of the metabolic syndrome: an American heart association/national heart, lung, and blood institute scientific statement. Circulation **112**, 2735–2752 (2005)
2. Mottillo, S., et al.: The metabolic syndrome and cardiovascular risk a systematic review and meta-analysis. J. Am. Coll. Cardiol. **56**, 1113–1132 (2010)
3. Zhang, L., Guo, Z., Wu, M., Hu, X., Xu, Y., Zhou, Z.: Interaction of smoking and metabolic syndrome on cardiovascular risk in a Chinese cohort. Int. J. Cardiol. **167**, 250–253 (2013)
4. Foster, K.R., Koprowski, R., Skufca, J.D.: Machine learning, medical diagnosis, and biomedical engineering research - commentary. Biomed. Eng. Online **13**, 94 (2014). https://doi.org/10.1186/1475-925X-13-94
5. Kononenko, I.: Machine learning for medical diagnosis: history, state of the art and perspective. Artif. Intell. Med. **23**(1), 89–109 (2001)
6. Zipf, G., Chiappa, M., Porter, K.S., Ostchega, Y., Lewis, B.G., Dostal, J.: National health and nutrition examination survey: plan and operations, 1999–2010. Vital Health Stat **1**(56), 1–37 (2013)
7. National Health and Nutrition Examination Survey data. Hyattsville (MD): US Department of Health and Human Services, Centers for Disease Control and Prevention, National Center for Health Statistics (2016). https://www.cdc.gov/Nchs/Nhanes/survey_methods.htm
8. Alberti, K.G., Zimmet, P., Shaw, J.: IDF epidemiology task force consensus group. The metabolic syndrome-a new worldwide definition. Lancet **366**(9491), 1059–1062 (2005). https://doi.org/10.1016/S0140-6736(05)67402-8
9. Zhu, F., et al.: Elevated blood mercury level has a non-linear association with infertility in US women: data from the NHANES 2013–2016. Reprod. Toxicol. **91**, 53–58 (2020)
10. Kohavi, R.: A study of cross-validation and bootstrap for accuracy estimation and model selection. IJCAI. **14**(2), 1137–1145 (1995)

A Comparative Study of ResNet and DenseNet in the Diagnosis of Colitis Severity

Chenxi Li[1], Jiawei Yang[1], Yuxin Qin[2], Lulu Lv[1], and Tao Li[1,3(✉)] (iD)

[1] College of Railway Transportation, Hunan University of Technology,
Zhuzhou, China
litao@hut.edu.cn
[2] School of Computing Science, University of Glasgow, Glasgow, UK
[3] Department of Computer Science, University of Sheffield, Sheffield, UK

Abstract. The current diagnostic approaches for assessing the severity of colitis necessitate medical professionals or specialists to subjectively evaluate colitis colonoscopy images, relying extensively on their clinical expertise. The accuracy of these assessments is of utmost importance in guiding subsequent treatment strategies for individuals with colitis. Several deep learning models have demonstrated their efficacy in the domain of medical imaging, serving as dependable tools for visualizing and analyzing medical data. These models include deep learning-based models and convolution-based neural network models. This study aimed to assess the effectiveness of various convolution-based neural network models in diagnosing the severity of colitis. Specifically, the representative ResNet and DenseNet models were chosen for a comparative analysis. Four types of medical imaging images of colitis with different severity were selected for classification and diagnosis. The experimental results demonstrate that DenseNet outperforms ResNet in terms of efficiency and accuracy for diagnosing colitis severity. DenseNet achieves an accuracy rate of up to 80%, indicating the promising potential for its application in the field of medicine.

Keywords: ResNet · DenseNet · Deep Learning · Colitis · Diagnosis

1 Introduction

Colitis is a pathological condition characterized by inflammation, which can be attributed to a multitude of etiological reasons. Diagnosis and treatment of colitis typically necessitate consideration of several aspects during the patient's visit. The incidence of consultations for colitis has had an upward trend in recent years. Nevertheless, it is important to acknowledge that the extent of colitis may be overestimated during the initial consultation, and failure to administer appropriate and timely treatment poses a significant risk of infection transmission, thereby significantly impacting the patient's overall well-being. Hence, it is imperative to precisely assess the extent of colitis by utilizing colonoscopy pictures during the initial stages of diagnosis with utmost accuracy and efficiency. This is crucial to prevent the potential issue of delayed therapy resulting from an underestimation of the patient's condition severity.

The diagnostic techniques commonly employed in medical practice to assess the severity of colitis typically involve the utilization of colonoscopy and mucosal biopsy. Colonic mucosal lesions are typically identified by physicians who rely on their own detection ability and clinical expertise. However, the reliance on clinicians alone for judging the severity of colitis is often seen as insufficient in terms of trustworthiness. The progressive advancement of deep learning is progressively emerging as a significant tool and instrument for paramedical care. Various deep learning models have demonstrated consistent performance in terms of their ability to withstand recognition and control systems, as well as exhibit rapid convergence [1,2]. In their study, Harada et al. [3] introduced a semi-supervised learning approach to categorize endoscopic images of colitis. Neural networks have been extensively utilized by researchers to classify medical images of diseases, including colitis [4,5]. These studies have demonstrated the effectiveness of employing deep learning techniques for the classification of colonoscopic images of colitis, thereby validating their potential utility in the clinical management of this condition.

In the realm of image classification, ResNet and DenseNet have demonstrated notable efficacy and achieved favorable outcomes. In their study, Sarwinda et al. [6] introduced a method for detecting colorectal cancer by employing ResNet-18 and ResNet-50 models, which yielded promising results in terms of accuracy. The DenseNet model has demonstrated exceptional performance in various domains such as daily life, agricultural output, and medical diagnostics. The severity of diabetic retinopathy was assessed using DenseNet by the authors in the paper [7]. The study conducted by the authors in reference [8] employed DenseNet as a methodology for the identification and categorization of diseases in tomato plant leaves.

This study aims to investigate the potential of deep learning in diagnosing disease severity and enhancing the performance of the colitis severity diagnostic model. To achieve this, the research employs two deep learning models, namely ResNet and DenseNet, for comparative analysis. Experimental evaluations are conducted to analyze the diagnostic outcomes of both models. The primary contributions of this study are as follows:

1. This study examines the disparities and dependability of two prominent convolution-based deep learning techniques, namely ResNet and DenseNet, within the domain of colitis severity diagnosis. The two models categorize colonoscopy images into four types based on the severity of colitis. This classification enhances the effectiveness of diagnosing colitis severity, minimizes the likelihood of subjective errors made by clinicians, and offers a framework for future investigations in the field of colitis severity diagnostic models.
2. A comparison analysis was conducted to assess the efficacy and performance of ResNet and DenseNet models in diagnosing the severity of colitis. The

study aimed to investigate the underlying mechanisms and classification accuracy of colonoscopy images using these two models. Subsequent investigations have demonstrated that DenseNet outperforms ResNet in the classification of colonoscopy images. This superiority is manifested not only in improved diagnosis accuracy but also in its superior generalization capabilities and processing economy.

2   Approach

2.1   The Diagnosis of Colitis Using a ResNet-Based Approach

The deep residual network (ResNet) is a deep learning model that was developed by He et al. [9]. Their research findings indicate that ResNet exhibits superior performance compared to other models in the task of image categorization. ResNet, in comparison to alternative deep learning models, effectively addresses the challenge of gradient vanishing or gradient explosion that arises from the deep network architecture by employing a residual structure. Additionally, ResNet exhibits reduced training time and computing cost, along with enhanced training capabilities.

The feature extraction process of the plain network may be demonstrated by utilizing the LIMUC dataset as the initial input data for training the model [10]

$$x_m = \sigma \left(\sum_{i=0}^{m} w_i x_i + \theta \right) \tag{1}$$

The symbol σ represents the non-linear activation function utilized in the neural network. The variable w_i represents the weight information associated with the colitis colonoscopy image, whereas x_i is the input data of said image. Lastly, θ denotes the bias term. To enhance the depth of the network while mitigating the issue of gradient explosion, the plain network incorporates a residual structure. The residual block can be created for every deep unit by employing recursive techniques. L characteristics are manifested as [9]

$$x_L = x_1 + \sum_{i=1}^{L-1} F(x_i, W_i) \tag{2}$$

In this context, L represents the unit layer of the neural network. $F(\cdot)$ represents the mapping relation of the residual structure. x_L refers to the output of the unit in the layer L, and x_i refers to the input of the unit in the layer i. In the context of backpropagation, given that the loss function is denoted as E, the application of the chain rule allows us to obtain the desired outcome

$$\frac{\partial E}{\partial x_1} = \frac{\partial E}{\partial x_L} \frac{\partial x_L}{\partial x_1} = \frac{\partial E}{\partial x_L} \left(1 + \frac{\partial}{\partial x_1} \sum_{i=1}^{L-1} F(x_i, w_i) \right) \tag{3}$$

The chain rule of backpropagation can be conceptually separated into two components. The first component involves the propagation of data signals without involving weight layers, which can be denoted as $\frac{\partial E}{\partial x_L}$. This process allows for the direct passage of data signals back to any shallow structure. The second component involves the propagation of data signals through weight layers, which can also be represented as $\frac{\partial E}{\partial x_L}(\frac{\partial}{\partial x_1}\sum_{i=1}^{L-1} F(x_i, w_i)). \frac{\partial E}{\partial x_L}(\frac{\partial}{\partial x_1}\sum_{i=1}^{L-1} F(x_i, w_i))$. This latter component ensures that the neural network model does not encounter the issue of vanishing gradient, as the resulting value cannot be equal to -1. In conclusion, the results generated by the Resnet-based colitis diagnostic network can be represented as

$$y = Softmax(F_L(R_{L-1}(F_{L-2}(\ldots(R_2(F_1(x; W_1, b_1)) + x_2; W_{R2}, b_{R2})\ldots) + x_{L-1}; W_{L-1}, b_{L-1})) + x_L; W_L, b_L) \tag{4}$$

In this context, the variable represents the severity of the colonists as recognized by the network by colonoscopy imaging. Additionally, Ri specifies the layer i residual block. The diagram illustrating the ResNet-based diagnostic model for assessing the severity of colitis is depicted in Fig. 1.A.

2.2   The Diagnosis of Colitis Using a DenseNet-Based Approach

The DenseNet model, initially introduced by G Huang et al. [11], is characterized by its dense connectivity. The DenseNet architecture incorporates the DenseBlock-Transition structure, which facilitates the connection of features across layers rather than relying on a linear mapping relationship. By utilizing colonoscopy images depicting colitis as the input data for model recognition, it is possible to articulate the relationship between the features of the input and the corresponding output [12].

$$X(t) = H([X0, X1, X2, ..., X(t-1)]) \tag{5}$$

Let $X(t)$ represent the output of layer t. $X0, X1, X2, ..., X(t-1)$ refer to the input data preceding layer t. H signifies the non-linear transformation applied to each DenseBlock. A DenseBlock refers to a module of many levels, wherein the feature maps of each layer possess identical dimensions. The Transition module serves the purpose of connecting two adjacent DenseBlocks, facilitating the reduction in the size of feature maps and ensuring their compatibility in terms of dimensionality through the utilization of Pooling. The diagnostic identification of four distinct forms of colitis with varying degrees of severity can be achieved by the utilization of the softmax function.

$$y = \text{Softmax}(F_{\text{output}}(F_{\text{avg-pool}}((F_{db}(x; W_{db}, b_{db})); W_{\text{avg-pool}}, b_{\text{avg-pool}}); W_{\text{output}}, b_{\text{output}}) \tag{6}$$

where y denotes the probability distribution of the outcome of the prediction of the severity course of colitis colonoscopy. F_{output} denotes the last fully connected layer of the model, the W_{output} and b_{output} denote their corresponding weights and biases. $F_{\mathrm{avg-pool}}$ denotes the average pooling layer of the model, and its corresponding associated weights and biases are $W_{\mathrm{avg-pool}}$ and $b_{\mathrm{avg-pool}}$. F_{db} denotes the different DenseBlocks, and the corresponding weights and biases of each DenseBlocks are W_{db} and b_{db}. The resulting DenseNet-based diagnostic model for colitis severity is shown in Fig. 1.B.

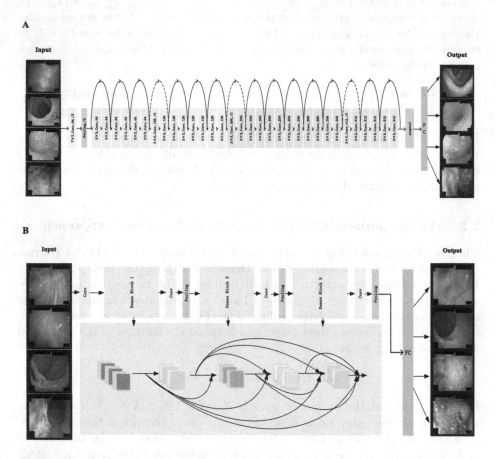

Fig. 1. A is the diagnosis of colitis using a ResNet-based approach; B is the diagnosis of colitis using a DenseNet-based approach

3   Experiments

The experimental patients for this investigation were picked from the LIMUC dataset [13], consisting of colonoscopy pictures depicting various colitis disorders. These diseases were classified into four severity classifications, namely Mayo 0, Mayo 1, Mayo 2, and Mayo 3. Out of the total 7502 data photos belonging to various classes, around 80% of these images, amounting to around 6000, were utilized as the training set in the conducted trials. Approximately 20% of the total number of photos, specifically around 1500 images, were allocated for utilization as the test set. To ensure equal representation of images for colitis illness identification in each acquisition, a consistent batch size of 16 was employed for the tests.

To assess the precision of the two network models in detecting colitis disease in colonoscopy images, we conducted tests on ResNet, and DenseNet, and pre-trained processed ResNet and DenseNet. As depicted in (a) of Fig. 2, the maximum accuracy achieved by the pre-trained DenseNet model is around 80%, while the maximum accuracy attained by the DenseNet model without pre-training is approximately 76%. The maximum accuracy achieved by the pre-trained ResNet model is approximately 73%, while the maximum accuracy attained by the ResNet model without pre-training is approximately 71%. The analysis demonstrates that DenseNet diverges from the conventional approach of increasing the depth and width of network layers to enhance model performance, as observed in ResNet. Instead, DenseNet achieves this by reducing the number of network parameters through the utilization of feature reuse and bypass mechanisms. This design choice not only facilitates training in comparison to ResNet but also yields a certain degree of regularisation effect. The pre-trained model has superior overall performance compared to the non-pre-trained model. Additionally, in the context of colitis illness detection, the pre-trained DenseNet exhibits faster convergence and more accurate analysis and identification of the severity of the disease.

The boxplot in Fig. 2(b) demonstrates that DenseNet exhibits superior performance compared to ResNet in terms of stability and accuracy across multiple experiments. This can be attributed to DenseNet's effective utilization of feature reuse, which prevents excessive weight shifting during training iterations. Consequently, the weights in DenseNet remain more stable throughout the training process, leading to improved overall stability when compared to the ResNet model.

Figure 2(c) compares the loss values of ResNet, DenseNet, and pre-trained processed ResNet and DenseNet in the context of feature detection in colitis colonoscopy images. The results indicate that DenseNet exhibits a notable advantage over ResNet in terms of both image feature detection and model robustness. Furthermore, the pre-trained DenseNet demonstrates superior capability in feature extraction specifically in the context of colitis. The pre-trained DenseNet demonstrates superior capability in extracting features from colitis colonoscopy images.

In Fig. 2(d), the histogram illustrates the minimum loss observed in colitis enteroscopy images for pathology detection using various models. The figure demonstrates that DenseNet, with its feature reuse and dense connectivity, effectively reduces the image loss in each iteration. Specifically, the loss value in colitis enteroscopy images can be reduced to approximately 0.5 for DenseNet without pre-training. Additionally, the pre-trained model exhibits a further reduction in loss value. The loss value of the pre-trained DenseNet model is 0.234. The untrained ResNet has a loss value of 0.347, whereas the pre-trained ResNet demonstrates a loss value almost equal to 0.239. The utilization of a pre-trained model has the potential to enhance the precision of picture classification and detection. Additionally, it can concurrently diminish the loss value associated with the identified image, as evidenced by the data presented in Fig. 2. While both pretrained DenseNet and ResNet exhibit identical loss outcomes, it is noteworthy that DenseNet demonstrates a greater accuracy. This observation suggests that DenseNet possesses superior robustness and generalization capabilities in comparison to ResNet.

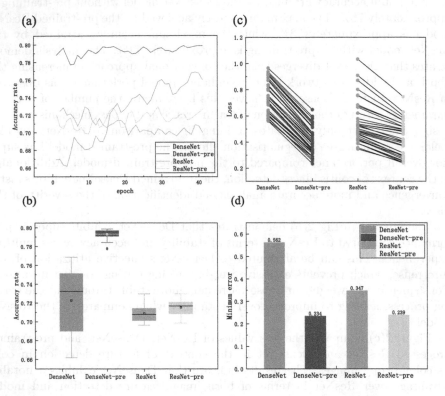

Fig. 2. (a) denotes the accuracy plot of ResNet and DenseNet under the LIMUC dataset; (b) denotes the boxplot obtained from multiple experiments of ResNet and DenseNet; (c) denotes the loss comparison between pre-trained and untrained ResNet and DenseNet; and (d) denotes the loss bar graph of ResNet and DenseNet loss histogram for LIMUC dataset detection

4   Conclusion

This study aimed to compare the performance of the two representative convolution based deep learning models, ResNet and DenseNet, in colonoscopy image classification. A series of comparative experiments were conducted to determine the viability of the two models in the diagnosis of colitis severity. According to the experimental results, DenseNet not only has a slight improvement in accuracy to reach 80% on colonoscopy images of colitis but also has a higher training efficiency of the model, which can reach convergence at a faster rate. ResNet and DenseNet both have strong feature extraction capabilities and image classification advantages. Therefore, DenseNet performs satisfactorily and has more advantages over ResNet in terms of diagnostic accuracy and robustness when it comes to determining the severity of colitis.

The comparative study may further examine the diagnostic performance and accuracy of the two models for colitis severity diagnosis. The deep learning model has the potential to be further developed in the diagnosis of the severity of colitis, as evidenced by the positive results of ResNet and DenseNet. Clinicians can use it as a practical tool to create personalized treatment plans that take into account the unique circumstances of each patient. Further investigation into ResNet and DenseNet will be carried out to address further obstacles in the processing of colonoscopy images from enterocolitis. To continuously enhance the performance of the colitis severity diagnostic model, more deep learning models will be tested and modified in this direction in the future. In the meantime, the application of deep learning models to the diagnosis of colitis severity has a promising development space.

References

1. Liu, K., Wang, R.: Antisaturation adaptive fixed-time sliding mode controller design to achieve faster convergence rate and its application. IEEE Trans. Circuits Syst. II Exp. Briefs **69**(8), 3555–3559 (2022)
2. Liu, K., Yang, P., Wang, R., Jiao, L., Li, T., Zhang, J.: Observer-based adaptive fuzzy finite-time attitude control for quadrotor UAVs. IEEE Trans. Aerosp. Electron. Syst. **59**(6), 8637–8654 (2023). https://doi.org/10.1109/TAES.2023.3308552
3. Harada, S., Bise, R., Hayashi, H., Tanaka, K., Uchida, S.: Order-guided disentangled representation learning for ulcerative colitis classification with limited labels. In: de Bruijne, M., et al. (eds.) MICCAI 2021. LNCS, vol. 12902, pp. 471–480. Springer, Cham (2021). https://doi.org/10.1007/978-3-030-87196-3_44
4. Alammari, A., Islam, A.R., Oh, J., Tavanapong, W., Wong, J., De Groen, P.C.: Classification of ulcerative colitis severity in colonoscopy videos using CNN. In: Proceedings of the 9th International Conference on Information Management and Engineering, pp. 139–144 (2017)
5. Bhambhvani, H.P., Zamora, A.: Deep learning enabled classification of mayo endoscopic subscore in patients with ulcerative colitis. Eur. J. Gastroenterol. Hepatol. **33**(5), 645–649 (2021)
6. Sarwinda, D., Paradisa, R.H., Bustamam, A., Anggia, P.: Deep learning in image classification using residual network (ResNet) variants for detection of colorectal cancer. Procedia Comput. Sci. **179**, 423–431 (2021)
7. Farag, M.M., Fouad, M., Abdel-Hamid, A.T.: Automatic severity classification of diabetic retinopathy based on DenseNet and convolutional block attention module. IEEE Access **10**, 38299–38308 (2022)

8. Albahli, S., Nawaz, M.: DCNet: DenseNet-77-based CornerNet model for the tomato plant leaf disease detection and classification. Front. Plant Sci. **13**, 957961 (2022)
9. He, K., Zhang, X., Ren, S., Sun, J.: Deep residual learning for image recognition. In: Proceedings of the IEEE Conference on Computer Vision and Pattern Recognition, pp. 770–778 (2016)
10. Kiranyaz, S., Avci, O., Abdeljaber, O., Ince, T., Gabbouj, M., Inman, D.J.: 1D convolutional neural networks and applications: a survey. Mech. Syst. Sig. Process. **151**, 107398 (2021)
11. Huang, G., Liu, Z., Van Der Maaten, L., Weinberger, K.Q.: Densely connected convolutional networks. In: Proceedings of the IEEE Conference on Computer Vision and Pattern Recognition, pp. 4700–4708 (2017)
12. Zhang, C., et al.: ResNet or DenseNet? Introducing dense shortcuts to ResNet. In: Proceedings of the IEEE/CVF Winter Conference on Applications of Computer Vision, pp. 3550–3559 (2021)
13. Polat, G., Kani, H., Ergenc, I., Alahdab, Y., Temizel, A., Atug, O.: Labeled images for Ulcerative Colitis (LIMUC) dataset, March 2022

Removal of EOG Artifact in Electroencephalography with EEMD-ICA: A Semi-simulation Study on Identification of Artifactual Components

Jingzhou Xu, Wengyao Jiang, Wei Wang, Jianjun Chen,
Yixiao Shen, and Jun Qi$^{(\boxtimes)}$

Xi'an Jiatong -Liverpool University, Renai Rd. 111, 215123 Suzhou, China
`jingzhou.xu@foxmail.com`,
`{wengyao.jiang20,yixiao.shen20}@student.xjtlu.edu.cn`,
`{Wei.Wang03,Jianjun.Chen,Jun.Qi}@xjtlu.edu.cn`

Abstract. Purpose: The electroencephalography (EEG) signals recorded in clinical settings are usually corrupted by electrooculography (EOG) artifacts. EEMD-ICA is a commonly used method for removing EOG artifacts. This study aims at exploring the performance of different methods of identification of artifactual components under the framework of EEMD-ICA.

Methods: This study is conducted in a semi-simulated way. A EEG dataset covering signal of SNR from -1 to 2 is generated based on the EEG and EOG segments from two public datasets. Characterized by the artifactual components identification method, EEMD-ICA$_{kurt}$, EEMD-ICA$_{entropy}$, EEMD-ICA$_{autocor}$ and EEMD-ICA$_{eogcor}$ are proposed and evaluated in terms of Normalized Mean Square Error (NMSE), Cross Correlation (CC) and Structural Similarity Index (SSIM) on this dataset.

Results: EEMD-ICA$_{autocor}$ outperforms other three approaches and demonstrates the strongest versatility. Besides successfully eliminating EOAs from EEG signals, it loses the least neuron activities.

Conclusion: Although performance metrics improve as SNR increases, the loss of structure information also improves (SNR > 1). In practice, it is vital to estimate the SNR of data before applying these approaches because when SNR is high, these methods may have a counterproductive.

Keywords: EEG · Artifact · Removal · EEMD · ICA

1 Introduction

Analyzing neural activities using Electroencephalography (EEG) plays a important role in neuroscience. It provides a non-invasive way to understand brain

Supported by Young Scientists Fund of the National Natural Science Foundation of China (Grant No. 62301452) and Natural Science Foundation of the Jiangsu Higher Education Institutions of China-General Programme (Grant No. 21KJB510024).

J. Qi and P. Yang (Eds.): IoTBDH 2023, CCIS 2019, pp. 111–123, 2024.
https://doi.org/10.1007/978-3-031-52216-1_10

dynamics and pathology. Clinically, EEG is crucial in the study and diagnosis of extensive kinds of diseases such as meningitis, encephalitis and brain parasites. EEG with iconic waveform can make doctors diagnose with clinical symptoms. In the therapeutic setting, EEG can be used to identify and treat epilepsy [15], research sleep and identify insomnia. In cognitive research, EEG is used to investigate cognitive processes like attention, memory, and emotion as well as human-computer interfaces like brain-computer interfaces (BCI).

Artifacts are undesired signals that get mixed into the data collected from the recording system, which can negatively impact the quality of the EEG signal and make its analysis more challenging especially on wearable devices [16], making it difficult for doctors to identify and use [14]. It may cause difficulties in reading, which make the diagnosis difficult to determine, and even lead to diagnostic errors. Even worse, some sophisticated computer instruments cannot detect EEG precisely under the interference of artifacts artifacts. The artifacts also bring difficulties of artificial intelligence in this field [23,26,27].

Generally, artifacts in EEG can be categorized into two types: non-physiological and physiological. Non-physiological artifacts are caused by subjects' misconduct, such as electrode displacement and body movement during recording. By providing proper subject instructions and experimental setup, non-physiological artifacts can be reduced [12]. Nevertheless, physiological artifacts cannot be avoided during EEG data collection. Physiological artifacts mainly refer to ocular artifacts, cardiac artifacts, and muscle artifacts [18]. One of the most common artifacts influencing the quality of EEG signals are the EOG Artifacts (EOAs), a kind of activities whose magnitude is usually much higher than that of EEG signals. Physiological artifacts can hardly be avoided during recording because they arise from the normal physiological activities of subjects.

As a result, identifying and removing artifacts, whether in clinical diagnosis or practical applications, is the most crucial prepossessing step before further analysis. Regression methods are the conventional approach for reducing artifacts from EEG [10], while Blind Source Separation (BSS) is one of the most commonly used techniques for removing physiological artifacts [8,12]. Blind source separation is a family of algorithms aiming at separating a set of source signals S from a set of signals formed by the mixture of S without the aid of information about S or the mixing process. Independent component analysis (ICA)-based methods are most commonly used for artifact removal [4,5] among BSS algorithms. Empirical Mode Decomposition (EMD) is another signal decomposition algorithm commonly used in EEG artifact removal and it is often combined with ICA in last decade, i.e., the EEMD-ICA [13].

EEMD-ICA is a kind of hybrid artifact removal technique [12]. The nature of EEMD allow this method to be used on both single channel and multi-channel EEG signal. Strictly speaking, EEMD-ICA is merely a tool for decomposing signals, and the most crucial step is to identify artifactual components. Therefore, this study aims at exploring the performance of different methods of identification of artifactual components under the framework of EEMD-ICA. By comprehensively testing four different ways of artifactual component identification, it is indicated the method based autocorrelation has the best performance. This study also draw a preliminary conclusion that, from the perspective of performance metrics, these artifact removal methods may have a counterproductive when SNR is high.

2   Methods

In this section, we first outline the various techniques employed in the paper and then we will describe the artifactual components identification method.

2.1   Blind Source Separation (BSS)

Blind source separation (BSS) is the one of the most used techniques to remove physiological artifacts [12,19]. Blind source separation is a family of algorithms, aiming at separating a set of source signals S from a set of signals formed by the mixture of S without the aid of information about S or the mixing process. Let X be the multi-channel EEG signals with linear mixture S, A be arbitrary mixing matrix, then mathematically,

$$X = AS, \tag{1}$$

in this way, an un-mixing matrix W can be generated by BBS to separate original sources,

$$\hat{S} = WX \tag{2}$$

where is the W is the estimation of the original source.

Numerous BSS techniques, such as independent component analysis (ICA), principal component analysis (PCA), canonical correlation analysis (CCA), and Empirical Mode Decomposition (EMD), have been developed to eliminate artifacts from EEG data.

2.2   Independent Component Analysis (ICA)

Independent component analysis (ICA) based methods are dominant for artifact removal [4,5] among BSS algorithms. ICA separates sources of signal from the raw signal and classifies them into the corresponding independent components (ICs). Raw signal can also be restored from ICs via Inverse-ICA. As shown in Fig. 1, after unmixing the raw multi-channel EEG signal into n ICs. Components which are not from neuronal activity will be rejected. Artifact- free EEG can be got via applying Inverse-ICA to remaining ICs.

Although ICA is a powerful tool for artifact removal, it has two major constraints. (a) ICA by its nature requires the channel number of input signal to be larger than the number of sources. If this requirement is not met, it may fail to separate the artifacts from the neural components [8]. (b) To generate reliable decomposition, ICA requires the input signal to have adequate samples. To undergo ICA decomposition on an EEG recording, it is presently recommended that the recording should has at least 30*(the number of input channels)^2 data samples [7].

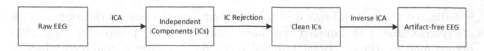

Fig. 1. The general design Of ICA-based artifact removal method. The artifact-free signal is recovered from remaining ICs after rejecting artifactual ones.

2.3   Empirical Mode Decomposition (EMD)

Empirical Mode Decomposition (EMD) is another BSS algorithm used in EEG artifact removal. EMD receives single channel signal and decompose it into intrinsic mode functions (IMFs) and a residual in an iteration way:

$$x(t) = \sum_{i=1}^{N} imf_i(t) + r_n(t) \tag{3}$$

where r_n is the residual when N IMFs have been extracted. The process of extracting IMFs stop when halting requirements are achieved or target number of IMFs have been got. Compared with other signal decomposition methods like ICA and PCA, EMD is a more robust method since it has no requirements on input signal. Although EMD can be used independently [11], it is often used to expand the channel number of EEG signal. So that the EEG record with few channels can also work with ICA and CCA [3,24].

One disadvantage of the EMD method is its susceptibility to noise, which leads to mode mixing issues [22].In the introduction of the specifics of the enhanced-EMD (EEMD) method [21], the robustness of EMD was increased by using the average of many ensembles of EMD as the ideal IMFs. In some circumstances, the remaining IMFs that have been rebuilt can be introduced into a separate environment for artifact removal to improve the quality of the EEG data.

2.4   EEMD-ICA

The idea of combining EEMD and ICA was first introduced to the task of EEG artifact removal in 2010 [13]. The research team behind this paper explored the theoretically best performance of EEMD-ICA yet their method can hardly be used in practical situation. Multiple improved methods have been put forward during past decades [1,24] to make EEMD-ICA an automatic artifact removal method. In spite of having various variants, the general idea of this method remains unified. As shown in Fig. 2, the paradigm is concise - Decompose raw signal, reject artifactual components and reconstruct artifact-free EEG signal. The main difference between variants of EEMD-ICA lies in the rules of component rejection, in other words, the method to identify artifactual components.

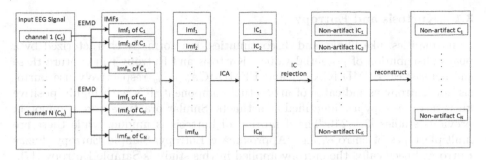

Fig. 2. The framework Of EEMD-ICA artifact removal method. This Figure consists of four committed steps (1) Decomposition of neural data with EEMD. (2) Artifact concentration with ICA. (3) Identification and rejection of artifactual components. (4) Signal reconstruction with remaining components.

2.5 Description of Simulated EEG Data

In this paper, the generation of simulated EEG data is based on EEG and EOG segments from two public datasets [9, 25]. The EOG artifacts is considered as a combination of Horizontal EOG (HEOG) and Vertical EOG (VEOG) [6]:

$$Artifact_{EOG} = \mu x_{HEOG} + \epsilon x_{VEOG} \tag{4}$$

where μ and ϵ respectively represents the contribution of HEOG and VEOG. Sufficient kinds of EOG artifacts can be generated by adjusting the coefficients, HEOG and VEOG. The artifactual EEG signal $EEG_{Contaminated}$ is then generated by mixing up $Artifact_{EOG}$ and EEG_{Pure}:

$$EEG_{Contaminated} = EEG_{Pure} + a(\mu \cdot HEOG + \epsilon \cdot VEOG) \tag{5}$$

where a represents the contribution of artifact. Hence, the signal to noise ratio (SNR) of $EEG_{Contaminated}$ can be denoted as:

$$SNR = 10 \log_{10} \frac{RMS(EEG_{Pure})}{RMS(a \cdot Artifact_{EOG})} \tag{6}$$

When EEG_{Pure} and $Artifact_{EOG}$ are determined. The SNR of generated $EEG_{Contaminated}$ can be controlled by adjusting coefficient a.

3 Identification of Artifactual Components

This study aim at exploring the performance of four kinds of EEMD-ICA related artifact removal method. Characterized by the artifactual components identification methods, these approaches are denoted as EEMD-ICA$_{kurt}$, EEMD-ICA$_{entropy}$, EEMD-ICA$_{autocor}$ and EEMD-ICA$_{eogcor}$

3.1   Kurtosis and Entropy

Abnormalities, like blinks and discontinuities, are normally characterized by a peaky distribution of potential values. Kurtosis and Entropy can capture these characteristics. EEMD-ICA$_{kurt}$ and EEMD-ICA$_{entropy}$ respectively use kurtosis and entropy as indicator of artifactual component. ICs with highly positive kurtosis or entropy are identified as artifacts. Similar practices were common in previous studies [3,5,24]. The definition of kurtosis is unique, while there are multiple types of entropy, e.g., Approximate Entropy, Sample Entropy, Fuzzy Entropy. Specifically, the entropy applied in this study is Sample Entropy [17].

3.2   Autocorrelation

Autocorrelation is used to describe the correlation degree of data itself in different periods, that is, to measure the influence of historical data on the present:

$$ACF(k) = \rho_k = \frac{\mathrm{Cov}\,(y_t, y_{t-k})}{\mathrm{Var}\,(y_t)} \qquad (7)$$

With the independent variable k representing the lag, the autocorrelation function (ACF) of a signal thus reflects its correlation with itself at different lags. In accordance to previous study [2], ocular artifacts are assumed to show higher autocorrelation. As shown in Fig. 3, The ACF of artifactual components in this study has obvious features. In the proposed EEMD-ICA$_{autocor}$ method, if the ACF of IC has higher energy, this IC is identified as artifactual component.

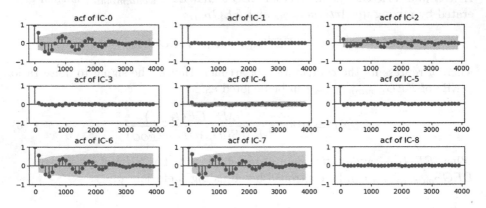

Fig. 3. An example of Autocorrelation Functions (ACFs) of ICs decomposed by EEMD-ICA. The ACF of IC 0, 2, 6, 7 obviously shows feature of tailing off to zero, indicating that these three components correspond to EOG artifact.

3.3   Correlation with EOG Reference Channel

When it comes to rejecting ocular artifact with BSS-based method, EOG Reference Channel is often introduced. Since BSS-based method can concentrate artifact into IC, it is assumed that the ICs correspond to ocular artifact have higher correlation with EOG reference channel. If EOG is not available, the EEG channel near the eyes can also be used as EOG reference channel. In a study that combine CCA and MEMD for EEG artifact removal, correlation with EOG reference channel is used to identify EOG artifacts [19]. In the proposed EEMD-ICA$_{eogcor}$ method, correlation of each IC of this EEG segment with EEG_{Pure} is calculated. The IC having higher correlation with original signal is identified as artifactual component (Fig. 4).

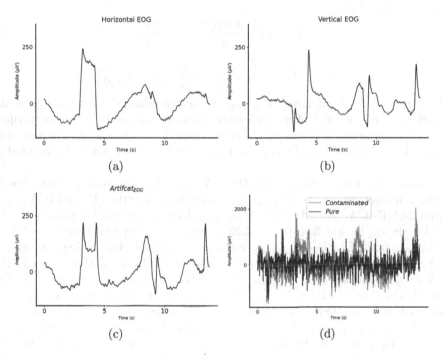

Fig. 4. An example of EEG simulation. (a) a segment of HEOG (b) a segment of VEOG (c) An example of $Artifact_{EOG}$ generated using Eq. 4 with $\mu = 1$, $\epsilon = 1$ (d) An example of $EEG_{Contaminated}$ generated using Eq. 6 with SNR = -1

4   Results and Discussion

To evaluate the performance of 4 artifact removal methods, we simulated 30 groups of single-channel corrupted EEG segments and each group contained 50 EEG segments. EEG segments within the same group were controlled to share unified SNR via the method in Sect. 2.5. To measure the influence SNR could have on the performance of artifact removal methods. Data of SNRs ranging from -1 to 2 by step 0.1 (except 0) were generated for testing. To comprehensively quantify the performance, we use three kinds of performance metrics. The Normalized Mean Square Error (NMSE) is the most commonly used metric for quantifying the difference between ground truth x and predicted value $\hat{x}$.

$$NMSE = \frac{\|x - \hat{x}\|_2^2}{\|x\|_2^2} \tag{8}$$

In this study, x is the artifact-free data EEG_{Pure}, $\hat{x}$ is the corresponding data reconstructed from the simulated artifactual signal EEG_{After}.

Another two metrics are the Cross Correlation (CC) and Structural Similarity Index (SSIM) [20]:

$$CC(x, \hat{x}) = \frac{Cov(x, \hat{x})}{\sigma_x \sigma_{\hat{x}}} = \frac{\sigma_{x\hat{x}}}{\sigma_x \sigma_{\hat{x}}} \tag{9}$$

$$SSIM(x, \hat{x}) = (\frac{2\mu_x \mu_{\hat{x}}}{\mu_x^2 + \mu_{\hat{x}}^2}) \cdot (\frac{2\sigma_x \sigma_{\hat{x}}}{\sigma_x^2 + \sigma_{\hat{x}}^2}) \cdot (\frac{\sigma_{x\hat{x}}}{\sigma_x \sigma_{\hat{x}}}) \tag{10}$$

where μ_x, $\mu_{\hat{x}}$ are local means and σ_x, $\sigma_{\hat{x}}$ are standard deviations. $\sigma_{x\hat{x}}$ is the covariance between x and $\hat{x}$. To better evaluate the contribution of artifact removal approaches, the variation of each metric is also taken into account. The results for every aritfactual component identification approach are presented in Fig. 5.

Among the four methods, EEMD-ICA$_{autocor}$ has the best performance in terms of all metrics. EEMD-ICA$_{entropy}$ is slightly weaker than EEMD-ICA$_{autocor}$ while EEMD-ICA$_{kurt}$ and EEMD-ICA$_{eogcor}$ have significant limitations.

As shown in Fig. 5 (a), the EEG data reconstructed through EEMD-ICA$_{autocor}$ and EEMD-ICA$_{entropy}$ remains a generally low NMSE, indicating higher similarity between reconstructed EEG and EEG_{Pure}. However, EEMD-ICA$_{entropy}$ is considered to be worse than EEMD-ICA$_{autocor}$ for two reasons. The overall NMSE of EEMD-ICA$_{entropy}$ is higher and its NMSE curve has intersection with baseline curve. The baseline curves represents the metrics calculated from $EEG_{Contaminated}$ and EEG_{Pure}, showing the values of the metrics when we were doing nothing. Having an intersection with baseline curve indicating that after the intersection point, applying this method is worse than doing nothing in terms of this metric. This intersection is called "critical point". For the figures in the upper row of Fig. 5, critical point is the intersection between curve and baseline curve. For the figures in lower row, critical point is the intersection between curve and horizontal zero line.

EEMD-ICA$_{kurt}$ and EEMD-ICA$_{eogcor}$ has a close overall performance in terms of NMSE while EEMD-ICA$_{kurt}$ has an advantage that its NMSE critical point appears later In terms of CC, although the performance of EEMD-ICA$_{kurt}$ and EEMD-ICA$_{eogcor}$ continuously improves with the increase of SNR, such trend is highly deceptive. As shown in Fig. 5 (e), the curves of these two methods are totally below horizontal 0 line and keep decreasing, indicating that

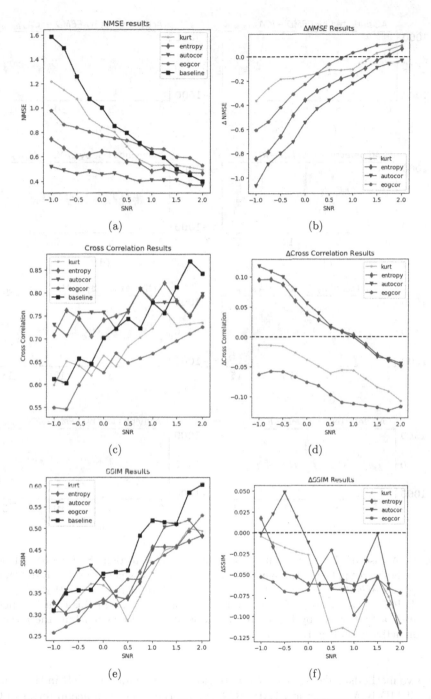

Fig. 5. The performance measures between different SNR for EEMD-ICA$_{kurt}$, EEMD-ICA$_{entropy}$, EEMD-ICA$_{autocor}$ and EEMD-ICA$_{eogcor}$, SNR of the synthetic data ranged from -1 (dB) to 2 (dB) with step 0.1 (dB). The diagrams in left column show the value of performance metrics and the diagrams in right column show the variation of performance metrics caused by applying different artifact removal approaches. (a) NMSE (b) ΔNMSE (c) CC (d) ΔCC (e) SSIM (f) ΔSSIM

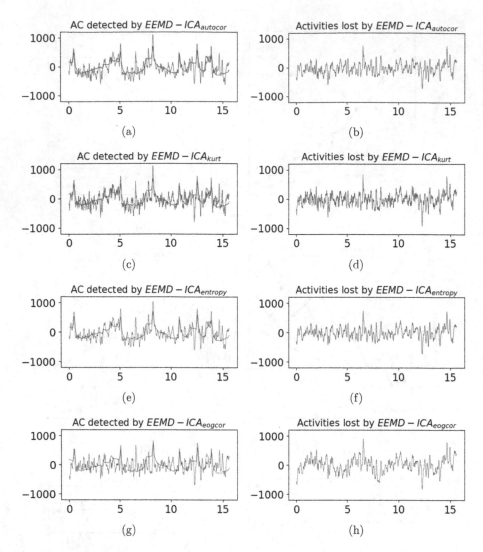

Fig. 6. A case of the artifactual components (ACs) detection (SNR=1.5). All four approaches were applied to the same contaminated EEG segment (SNR = 1.5). (a), (c), (e), (g) are ACs detected by EEMD-ICA$_{autocor}$, EEMD-ICA$_{kurt}$, EEMD-ICA$_{entropy}$, EEMD-ICA$_{eogcor}$. (b), (d), (f), (h) are lost neuron activities. In this case, the power of neuron activities lost by EEMD-ICA$_{eogcor}$ is about twice as much as the power of neuron activities lost by EEMD-ICA$_{autocor}$

the two methods make negative contributions to CC under all SNR in this study. For EEMD-ICA$_{autocor}$ and EEMD-ICA$_{entropy}$, their performance in terms of CC are highly close. But their contribution to CC turn negative at around SNR = 1.0, indicating these two methods may not be suitable for high SNR signal.

As shown in 5 (c), (f), four approaches all cause decrease of SSIM under most SNR. This may mean that EEMD-ICA based artifact removal process inevitably lead to loss of structural information. This is probably because the ICs identified as artifacts still contains components from normal neural activities. Relatively speaking, EEMD-ICA$_{autocor}$ performs best in terms of SSIM. As presented in Fig. 6, EEMD-ICA$_{autocor}$ has the least neuron activities loss. Considering NMSE, CC and SSIM comprehensively, EEMD-ICA$_{autocor}$ is the artifact removal approach of best performance among the four proposed approaches.

5   Conclusion

This study developed four EEMD-ICA based approaches to artifact rejection for noisy neural data: EEMD-ICA$_{kurt}$, EEMD-ICA$_{entropy}$, EEMD-ICA$_{autocor}$ and EEMD-ICA$_{eogcor}$. These approaches share the signal decomposition procedure while differ in terms of artifactual components identification method. The effectiveness of proposed approaches were examined with semi-simulated data.

When using NMSE as the metric, EEMD-ICA$_{autocor}$ significantly outperformed the other two approach. It can almost be twice as good as EEMD-ICA$_{entropy}$. When the SNR was high, the difference between the four approaches was reduced in terms of absolute NMSE value. However, all methods except EEMD-ICA$_{autocor}$ shows negative contribution to NMSE when SNR was high. When SNR is larger than 1.0, EEMD-ICA$_{eogcor}$ resulted worse NMSE than doing nothing while such phenomenon appeared when SNR is larger than 1.5 for EEMD-ICA$_{entropy}$ and EEMD-ICA$_{kurt}$. It is indicated that EEMD-ICA$_{autocor}$ shown best versatility.

When using CC as the metric. The performance of EEMD-ICA$_{eogcor}$ and EEMD-ICA$_{kurt}$ were unacceptable for their negative contribution to CC under all SNR. While EEMD-ICA$_{autocor}$ and EEMD-ICA$_{entropy}$ had close performance. In terms of CC, these two approaches are only suitable for data with SNR being less than 1.0. When using SSIM as the metric, all the four approaches have poor performance. Although performance improved as SNR increased. These approaches contributed negatively to SSIM.

Generally speaking, EEMD-ICA$_{autocor}$ and EEMD-ICA$_{entropy}$ are effective in artifact removal. However, a significant drawback of these methods is that they show worse performance than the baseline when the SNR is high, limiting their scope of application to severely contaminated EEG signal.

Effectiveness of the four artifact rejection approaches had been evaluated and these approaches can act as prepossessing and improve the performance of following task. However, it is vital to estimate the SNR of data before applying these approaches because when SNR is high, these methods may have a counterproductive effect.

References

1. Bai, Y., et al.: Reduction hybrid artifacts of EMG-EOG in electroencephalography evoked by prefrontal transcranial magnetic stimulation. J. Neural Eng. **13**(6), 066016 (2016). https://doi.org/10.1088/1741-2560/13/6/066016

2. Chen, X., et al.: Simultaneous ocular and muscle artifact removal from EEG data by exploiting diverse statistics. Comput. Biol. Med. **88**, 1–10 (2017). ISSN: 0010–4825. https://doi.org/10.1016/j.compbiomed.2017.06.013, https://www.sciencedirect.com/science/article/pii/S0010482517301774

3. Chen, X., et al.: The use of multivariate EMD and CCA for denoising muscle artifacts from few-channel EEG recordings. IEEE Trans. Instrum. Measur. **67**(2), 359–370 (2017)

4. Delorme, A., Makeig, S.: EEGLAB: an open source toolbox for analysis of single-trial EEG dynamics including independent component analysis. **134**(1), 9–21 (2004). https://doi.org/10.1016/J.JNEUMETH.2003.10.009

5. Delorme, A., Sejnowski, T., Makeig, S.: Enhanced detection of artifacts in EEG data using higher-order statistics and independent component analysis. NeuroImage **34**(4), 1443–1449 (2007). ISSN: 1053–8119. https://doi.org/10.1016/j.neuroimage.2006.11.004, https://www.sciencedirect.com/science/article/pii/S1053811906011098

6. Elbert, T., et al.: Removal of ocular artifacts from the EEG – a biophysical approach to the EOG. Electroencephalogr. Clin. Neurophysiol. **60**(5), 455–463 (1985). ISSN: 0013–4694. https://doi.org/10.1016/0013-4694(85)91020-X, https://www.sciencedirect.com/science/article/pii/001346948591020X

7. Gabard-Durnam, L.J., et al.: The harvard automated processing pipeline for electroencephalography (HAPPE): standardized processing software for developmental and high-artifact data. Front. Neurosci. **12**, 97 (2018)

8. Jiang, X., Bian, G.B., Tian, Z.: Removal of artifacts from EEG signals: a review. Sensors **19**(5), 987 (2019)

9. Klados, M.A., Bamidis, P.D.: A semi-simulated EEG/EOG dataset for the comparison of EOG artifact rejection techniques. Data Brief **8**, 1004–1006 (2016). ISSN: 2352–3409. https://doi.org/10.1016/j.dib.2016.06.032, https://www.sciencedirect.com/science/article/pii/S2352340916304000

10. Klados, M.A., et al.: REG-ICA: a hybrid methodology combining blind source separation and regression techniques for the rejection of ocular artifacts. Biomed. Sig. Process. Control **6**(3), 291–300 (2011). ITAB 2009, ISSN: 1746–8094. https://doi.org/10.1016/j.bspc.2011.02.001, https://www.sciencedirect.com/science/article/pii/S1746809411000061

11. Looney, D., Li, L., Rutkowski, T.M., Mandic, D.P., Cichocki, A.: Ocular artifacts removal from EEG using EMD. In: Wang, R., Shen, E., Gu, F. (eds.) Advances in Cognitive Neurodynamics ICCN 2007, pp. 831–835. Springer, Dordrecht (2008). https://doi.org/10.1007/978-1-4020-8387-7_145

12. Mannan, M.M.N., Kamran, M.A., Jeong, M.Y.: Identification and removal of physiological artifacts from electroencephalogram signals: A review. IEEE Access **6**, 30630–30652 (2018). https://doi.org/10.1109/ACCESS.2018.2842082

13. Mijović, B., et al.: Source separation from single-channel recordings by combining empirical-mode decomposition and independent component analysis. IEEE Trans. Biomed. Eng. **57**(9), 2188–2196 (2010)

14. Minguillon, J., Lopez-Gordo, M.A., Pelayo, F.: Trends in EEG-BCI for daily-life: requirements for artifact removal. Biomed. Sig. Process. Control **31**, 407–

418 (2017). ISSN: 1746–8094. https://doi.org/10.1016/j.bspc.2016.09.005, https://www.sciencedirect.com/science/article/pii/S1746809416301318

15. Noachtar, S. and Rémi, J.: The role of EEG in epilepsy: a critical review. Epilepsy Behav. **15**(1), 22–33 (2009). ISSN: 1525–5050. https://doi.org/10.1016/j.yebeh.2009.02.035., https://www.sciencedirect.com/science/article/pii/S1525505009000924

16. Qi, J., et al.: An overview of data fusion techniques for internet of things enabled physical activity recognition and measure. Inf. Fusion **55** 269–280 (2020). ISNN: 1566–2535. https://doi.org/10.1016/j.inffus.2019.09.002, https://www.sciencedirect.com/science/article/pii/S1566253519302258

17. Simons, S., Espino, P., Abásolo, D.: Fuzzy entropy analysis of the electroencephalogram in patients with alzheimer's disease: is the method superior to sample entropy? Entropy **20**(1), 21 (2018). https://doi.org/10.3390/E20010021

18. Urigüen, J.A., Garcia-Zapirain, B.: EEG artifact removal–state-of the-art and guidelines. **3**(1), 031001 (2015). https://doi.org/10.1088/1741-2560/12/3/031001

19. Wang, G., et al.: The removal of EOG artifacts from EEG signals using independent component analysis and multivariate empirical mode decomposition. IEEE J. Biomed. Health Inf. **20**(5), 1301–1308 (2016). https://doi.org/10.1109/JBHI.2015.2450196

20. Wang, Z., et al.: Image quality assessment: from error visibility to structural similarity. IEEE Trans. Image Process. **13**(4), 600–612 (2004). https://doi.org/10.1109/TIP.2003.819861

21. Wu, Z., Huang, N.E.: Ensemble empirical mode decomposition: a noise-assisted data analysis method. Adv. Adapt. Data Anal. **1**(01), 1–41 (2009)

22. Xu, X., Chen, X., Zhang, Y.: Removal of muscle artefacts from few-channel EEG recordings based on multivariate empirical mode decomposition and independent vector analysis. Electron. Lett. **54**(14), 866–868 (2018)

23. Yang, P., et al.: Activity graph based convolutional neural network for human activity recognition using acceleration and gyroscope data. IEEE Trans. Ind. Inf. **18**(10), 6619–6630 (2022). https://doi.org/10.1109/TII.2022.3142315

24. Zeng, K., et al.: An EEMD-ICA approach to enhancing artifact rejection for noisy multivariate neural data. IEEE Trans. Neural Syst. Rehabil. Eng. **24**(6), 630–638 (2015)

25. Zhang, H., et al.: EEGdenoiseNet: a benchmark dataset for deep learning solutions of EEG denoising. J. Neural Eng. **18**(5), 056057 (2021). https://doi.org/10.1088/1741-2552/ac2bf8

26. Zhou, M., Yang, P.:. Automatic temporal relation in multi- task learning. In: Proceedings of the 29th ACM SIGKDD Conference on Knowledge Discovery and Data Mining, pp. 3570–3580 (2023)

27. Zhou, M., et al.: Robust temporal smoothness in multi-task learning. In: Proceedings of the AAAI Conference on Artificial Intelligence, vol. 37, no. 9. pp. 11426–11434 (2023)

Representative UPDRS Features of Single Wearable Sensor for Severity Classification of Parkinson's Disease

Yuting Zhao[1], Xulong Wang[2], Xiyang Peng[2], Ziheng Li[1], Fengtao Nan[1], Menghui Zhou[1], Peng Yue[2], Zhong Zhao[3], Yun Yang[1], and Po Yang[2]([✉])

[1] National Pilot School of Software, Yunnan University, Kunming, China
{zhaoyuting,liziheng9050}@mail.ynu.edu.cn, yangyun@ynu.edu.cn
[2] Department of Computer Science, University of Sheffield, Sheffield, UK
{xl.wang,xpeng24,pyue1,po.yang}@sheffield.ac.uk
[3] Yunnan First People's Hospital, Kunming, China

Abstract. Parkinson's disease (PD) is a common neurodegenerative disease. So far, there is no cure for this disease, but the right medicine can slow down the progress of the disease. Therefore, early diagnosis of this disease is very important to improve the quality of life of patients with PD. In recent years, wearable devices have been widely used to classify, predict and monitor the condition of patients with PD. Most previous studies extracted some features for classification, but due to the different research activities, the extracted features lack of standards and generality, when the activities change, the previously extracted features are not necessarily effective. In this paper, we differentiate the PD severity and select representative 20 features related to the disease. For this reason, we designed 8 commom activities and collect data of 85 PD patients using inertial wearable sensors off-the-shelf accelerometer, gyroscope sensors. Our best results demonstrate that the classification accuracy of PD severity is 81.37%. Therefore, this can play a role in assisting doctors in diagnosing and adjusting medication in a timely manner. Meanwhile, feature selection reduced the burden of the model and facilitate the later transplantation of lightweight devices.

Keywords: Parkinson's disease · Machine learning · Wearable sensor · Feature selection

1 Introduction

Parkinson's disease (PD) is the second most common neurodegenerative disease in the world [4], affecting more than 6 million people worldwide [7]. The common clinical motor symptoms of PD include muscle stiffness, tremor, motor retardation, and gait freezing [9]. These symptoms greatly affect the quality of life of patients. Therefore, the use of wearable devices to capture the patient's

J. Qi and P. Yang (Eds.): IoTBDH 2023, CCIS 2019, pp. 124–136, 2024.
https://doi.org/10.1007/978-3-031-52216-1_11

movement information to assist in diagnosing the disease has become a problem worthy of attention [31].

In recent years, many approaches have been developed to classify PD severity in clinical practice. Neuroimaging has been increasingly used as an objective method for the diagnosis of PD [19], but that's expensive and not conducive to observing the environment outside the hospital. At present, the other clinical scales standard for PD is the Unified Parkinson's Disease Rating Scale (UPDRS) [28], which is a qualitative assessment completed by the subjective judgment of neurologists. The UPDRS can be administered in daily clinical practice without any expensive equipment. However, the scales tend to be subjective and static. Neurologists record patient reactions during different tasks and assign ratings according to UPDRS requirements, it is time-consuming and influenced by the clinical experience of doctors. At the same time, doctors are only monitoring the current symptoms in the hospital and cannot conduct timely assessments outside the hospital or in other environments [2].

In order to develop objective criteria to facilitate timely estimation of the PD severity, utilising wearable sensors to monitor disease information inside and outside the hospital has received considerable critical attention [6,14,20,21,24, 26,30,34].

It is necessary to remotely monitor patients with PD and constantly check their symptoms in order to analyze their condition more effectively. The auxiliary diagnosis technology of PD based on wearable devices and machine learning can help individuals to detect the disease at an early stage, and also help doctors to monitor and evaluate patients inside and outside the hospital, so as to improve the accuracy of clinical diagnosis, patients. Additionally, it is helpful for timely and effective adjustment of treatment plans to reduce the economic burden on patients.

Machine learning (ML) is frequently used for medical disease diagnosis recently because of its implementation convenience and high accuracy [18,23,35]. Jin et al. [15] develop a quantitative measure of bradykinesia which can be conveniently used during clinical finger taps test in patients with PD. Four performance indices were derived from the gyrosensor sensor signal include root-mean-squared (RMS) angular velocity, RMS angular displacement, peak power and total power. The system of Patel et al. [21] used support vector machine (SVM) to distinguish PD patients from healthy controls based on accelerometer data. Five different types of features were estimated from the accelerometer data: the range of amplitude of each channel, the root mean square (rms) value of each accelerometer signal, two cross-correlation-based features, and two frequency-based features. Juberty et al. [10] explored extracting chest inclination leg agility from the shimmer device which was estimated using SVM and K nearest neighbor (KNN) for automatic UPDRS assessment. Aleksei et al. [27] differentiate healthy controls from patients with stages 1 and 2 PD by caculating time, correlation and frequency features, but they only conducted disease detection and did not conduct detailed disease severity. Guo et al. [12] collected walking data from 10 PD patients in a laboratory setting to diagnose the freezing of gait by using the freezing index. However, this research only detects a single motor symptom. Pérez-Ibarra et al. [22] collected data from 5 healthy adults and 7 patients with PD walking on a treadmill as well as on the floor under the guidance of a professional, they development a real-time adaptive unsupervised algorithms for identification of gait events and phases from a single IMU mounted at the back of the foot. Luis Sigcha et al. [29] used the inertial sensors embedded in consumer smartwatches and different ML models to detect bradykinesia in the upper extremities and evaluate its severity. Six PD subjects and seven age-matched healthy controls were equipped with a consumer smartwatch and asked to perform a set of motor exercises for at least 6 weeks. Chén et al. [5] based on smartphone sensors, extracting signals from patients performing the specified six activities at home, PD and healthy people are classified through an automated disease assessment framework. However, it does not take into account the abnormalities that arise when performing activities at home. To reduce the number of anomalies occurring in home data collection, Erb et al. [8,13] proposed a scheme that the patient logs were completed by caregivers to track patients' daily activities, PD symptoms, and medication intake. However, caregivers have a vague delineation of symptoms and are unable to correctly identify motor symptoms, which lead to misunderstandings and errors. Martin Ullrich et al. [32] collect data with inertial measurement units over two weeks from 12 patients with idiopathic PD who completed the series of three consecutive 4 × 10-Meters-Walking Tests at different walking speeds besides their usual daily-living activities.

Although the previous research has extracted several features that are effective for classification, these systems primarily focus on extracting common features specific to designated activities. When target activity is altered, features that were effective on the original activity may not remain superior on the new activity. Hence, our objective is to identify the most representative features for PD severity classification.

Targeting at above-mentioned issues, this article focuses on differentiate the PD severity and select representative 20 features related to the disease. More precisely, to ensure data reliability, we firstly collect 85 PD subjects of different severity grades. Each subject performs the 8 activities within the part-III of UPDRS scale and is scored by the movement disorders neurologists. Our experimental design is conducted from four perspectives. Firstly, we explore the impact of different window sizes on data processing, we segment the dataset using sliding windows and experiment with various window sizes such as 1 s, 1.5 s and 3 s. In the second step, we focus on model selection to test the robustness of features. We validate several mainstream machine learning models, including Support Vector Machine (SVM), Logistic Regression (LR), and LightGBM (LGBM). In the third step, we employ joint model feature selection(JMFS) mechanism to select common important feature. Our objective is to identify the most important common feature set among eight different types of activities. Lastly, we determine the optimal feature dimension by comparing the performance differences among different feature dimensions, such as 10, 20, 30, and so on. This enables us to select the feature dimension that exhibits the best performance. The experimental results show that when using the feature set extracted with a window size of 300, the first 20 important features selected through feature selection are 8.22% higher than using all features in the classification of PD severity.

The focus of this study is to assess the severity of patients with PD through single wearable sensor. Our contributions are as follows:

- A novel technical pipeline is proposed for fine-grained classification of PD severity and identifying the most representative features.
- The most representative 20 symptom-related features is presented in 8 UPDRS activities from gyroscope and accelerometer data.
- We provide ablation experiments on three aspects from model, window size and feature dimensions respectively to ensure the representative and generalisation of the proposed features.

The rest of this paper is arranged as follows. Section 2 describe the methods used in this work, We discuss the results of our research in Sect. 3. Finally, Sect. 4 summarizes this paper and put forward the future prospects.

Table 1. UPDRS Paradigm Activities

Num	Activity name	abbre
1	Finger taps	FT
2	Clench and open alternately	COA
3	Rapid alternating movements of hands	ALTER
4	Hand rotation-right	HR-R
5	Hand rotation-left	HR-L
6	Finger to nose-right	FN-R
7	Standing with arms hold	STANDH
8	Walk back and forth	WA

2   Methods

2.1   Data Acquisition

As part of the research, data were collected at Yunnan First People's Hospital (China). The study participants were informed about the project and signed a written consent form. The dataset consists of a total of 85 participants,18 with stage 1, 34 with stage 2, 19 with stage 3, 14 with stage 4, other informations(age: 64 ± 10, gender: 35 male, 24 female, height: 165 cm ± 10, weight: 56 kg ± 10). After negotiating and signing the data collection consent form, the experiment will start. Firstly, a inertial sensors will be worn on the patient's right wrist, then, under the guidance of professionals, patients are required to complete a series of 8 tasks in Table 1, which are selected from the UPDRS-III scale based on the advice of neurologists [11]. Each action collected for 20 s without special instructions, the duration of the entire procedure is approximately 6 min. Each task has a specific purpose, such as evoking specific symptoms of PD. Figure 1 shows 8 normal form activities.

2.2 Data Preprocessing and Feature Extraction

The activity data is collected by the wearable sensor shimmer 3 IMU units with a sampling frequency of 204 Hz which is synchronously transmitted to the computer through Bluetooth connection, its data include three-axis accelerometer and gyroscope signal. Raw data lines were written into a text file and then converted into a CSV format, with seven data columns: timestamp, x, y, and z-axis of the accelerometer and gyroscrope data.

In order to isolate the frequencies related to the disease and maintain the authenticity of the original signal to a greater extent and reduce the interference of noise, the original data is usually filtered and processed. Through signal spectrum analysis of the signals we collected and review of relevant literatures, the tremor frequency of PD patients can be divided into three categories: resting tremor 3–6 Hz, postural tremor 4–12 Hz and motor tremor 2–7 Hz [3]. Therefore, it is recommended to use a 3–12 Hz band-pass filter to filter the patient's motion signals. After filtering, the data of each axis are normalized by Z-score standardization [25]. After that, a sliding window will be used to segment the original time series data. The window division method is Semi-Non-Overlapping Window and the overlap rate is 50% [1]. The window size should include at least 2–3 activity cycles. In this study, the window size will be divided according to the minimum time point and peak width of the waveform [16]. Therefore, we select the sliding window size of 200, 300 and 600 to test an optimal window size, Fig. 2 shows using sliding windows of different sizes for feature extraction on the waveform of Activity 1 signal collected by the sensor.

After that,87 dimensional features are extracted from the accelerometer and gyroscope, and time domain features include: maximum, minimum, mean, variance, standard deviation, amplitude (X, Y, Z, A, T), skewness (X, Y, Z, A, T), kurtosis (X, Y, Z, A, T), autocorrelation coefficient maximum and minimum (X, Y, Z, A, T); frequency domain features include: maximum spectrum, mean (X, Y, Z, A, T), correlation coefficient (XY, XZ, XA, XT, YZ, YA, YT, ZA, ZT, AT), root mean square (X, Y, Z, A, T), energy values (X, Y, Z, A, T), Entropy (X, Y, Z, A, T), main frequency (A, T). A total of 174 dimensional features. X, Y and Z respectively represent the three axes of the three-dimensional sensor, A is the fusion axis of the three axes, T is the inclination axis, and the fusion representation of the three axes is performed by calculating the signal amplitude vector. For the fusion axis, the fusion representation of the three axes is performed by calculating the signal amplitude vector (SMV), which avoids the user's change in a single direction, which helps to measure the overall intensity of the activity.

Fig. 1. Eight Representative Paradigm Activities.

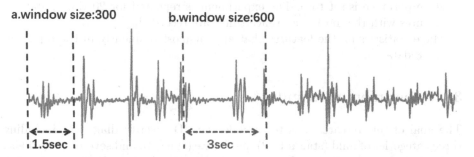

Fig. 2. Using sliding windows of different sizes for feature extraction on the waveform of Activity 1 signal collected by the sensor.

2.3   Representative Feature Selection

After feature extraction,significant feature selection is performed to select the most useful features for disease classification. Cause different models have different scales indexes of feature importance [17,33], and there are multiple ranking results of importance, so we consider using Joint Model Feature Selection (JMFS) mechanism to select common important features. We use SVM-L1, SVM-L2, LR-L1, LR-L2, LGBM a total of 5 models to make joint decisions.

The LGBM model has low computational complexity and good scalability in calculating the importance of features. Due to its framework based on gradient lifting trees, the calculation of feature importance is carried out by iteratively fitting residuals and selecting the best segmentation point, without being limited by feature dimensions. This makes LGBM suitable for processing large-scale datasets and high-dimensional features. The LR model is relatively simple in calculating the importance of features. Due to its linear nature, the importance of features can be measured by observing the absolute values of model parameters.

LR has low computational complexity and good scalability, making it suitable for tasks where feature importance is calculated. The SVM model is relatively complex in calculating the importance of features. The calculation of feature importance involves retraining the model and calculating support vectors, which may result in high computational complexity and limited scalability. Especially when dealing with large-scale datasets and high-dimensional features, SVM has a high requirement for calculating the importance of features.

SVM train the best hyperparameters from [0.0001,0.001, 0.01,0.1,1], LR train the best hyperparameters from [0.001,0.01,0.1,1,2], the learning rate of LGBM is 0.05, and the maximum depth of the tree is 2. The feature selection process is as follows:

- Input the samples into the model and sort the feature weights generated after training in descending order;
- Each time the feature weights are sorted in descending order, the 20th weight is taken as the threshold, the first 20 importance is set to 1, and the last 20 importance is set to 0. The experiment is repeated for 20 times, and the features with the most occurrence times are recorded;
- Make statistics on the features that appear most frequently in the top 20 of the 8 data sets.

3   Experimental Results

The goal of this research was to provide the PD severity diagnosis, including three categories of mild (stages 1+2), moderate (stage 3), and severe (stage 4+5), and select representative 20 features related to the disease. At the same time, we explored the most appropriate sliding window size and the optimal feature dimension. In this scope, it was decided to use three classification approaches taking a part of this work including differentiating between.

We validated our approach on datasets collected in a laboratory environment. All our experiments were carried out on an ordinary computer with 2.6G Hz CPU and 8 GB memory. Experiment metrics including accuracy, f1-score, precision and racll. LGBM classifiers was used in final since provided the best results.

3.1   Representative Features

We use the JMFS mechanism proposed in methods 2.3 to select important features for the extracted 174 dimensional features. Cause different models have different scales indexes of feature importance, and there are multiple ranking results of importance, JMFS mechanism can identify the most important features they share, so that the selected features can ensure robustness and universality. The final selected top 20 dimensional features are shown in the Fig. 3.

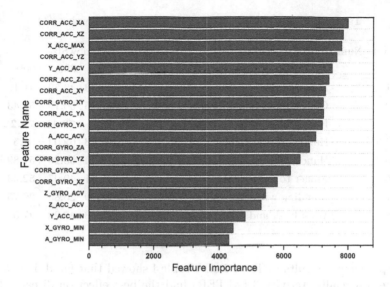

Fig. 3. Feature importance ranking. This figure shows the top 20 most important features jointly selected by the five models.

CORR represents axis correlation, ACV represents autocorrelation coefficient variance. From the top 20 most important features selected, CORR and ACV are features worth paying close attention to, followed by the maximum and minimum values of the x and y axes that play an important role. In addition, we also find that the features of the accelerometer correspond to those of the gyroscope.

3.2 Sliding Window Size

Table 2 shows the classification accuracy of 8 activities using different window size. We found that the window contains different periods and the key features extracted vary. From the experimental results, the most suitable window size is 300. For small amplitude actions, using a window of 300 is optimal. For larger amplitude activities such as Activity 6(FN-R), using a window of 600 will have slightly higher accuracy, possibly due to the fact that the window of 600 contains more activity cycles than the window of 300. As for window of 200, the reason for the average accuracy of the results is that it contains too few activity cycles and the model does not learn the motion laws well. Additionally, Window size has little effect on static activity such as Activity 8(STANDH).

3.3 Models

After determining the optimal window size, we conducted a fine-grained classification of PD severity, which refers to the three classifications of mild (stages 1+2), moderate (stage 3), and severe (stage 4+5). The highest accuracy is highlighted with bold and hand fine category activities are highlighted with underline.

Table 2. Classification accuracy of different windowsize (%)

Act_Num	Activity_Name	WindowSize		
		200	300	600
1	Finger taps	41.33	42.59	41.12
2	Clench and open alternately	58.45	60.19	59.43
3	Rapid alternating movements of hands	**72**	**73.15**	**72.22**
4	Hand rotation-right	62.03	62.04	61.5
5	Hand rotation-left	58.44	59.26	57.89
6	Finger to nose-right	48.21	49.07	52.33
7	Standing with arms hold	26.79	26.85	26.75
8	Walk back and forth	46.93	47.22	47.54

The experimental results in Table 3 and Table 4 showed that hand fine category activities especially Activity 3 (ALTER) had the best effect on disease classification reaching 73.15%.

Table 3. Classification result of PD severity (%)

Act_Num	Activity_Name	LGBM				SVM			
		Acc	F1	Pre	Rec	Acc	F1	Pre	Rec
1	FT	42.59±0.12	41.89±0.06	41.73±0.09	42.59±0.14	27.78±0.26	27.72±0.32	27.84±0.06	27.78±0.18
2	COA	60.19±0.07	59.55±0.11	59.9±0.03	60.19±0.03	52.78±0.19	52.96±0.16	56.5±0.10	52.78±0.21
3	ALTER	**73.15±0.03**	**72.99±0.01**	**73.42±0.11**	**73.15±0.07**	49.07±0.11	49.08±0.02	49.46±0.13	49.07±0.09
4	HR-R	62.04±0.13	62.03±0.20	62.6±0.05	62.03±0.12	55.56±0.07	55.87±0.18	56.46±0.21	55.56±0.16
5	HR-L	59.26±0.13	58.98±0.10	59.99±0.22	59.26±0.08	44.44±0.22	43.87±0.07	43.66±0.11	44.45±0.08
6	FN-R	52.78±0.09	52.74±0.17	53.94±0.08	52.78±0.06	35.19±0.13	34.1±0.06	34.76±0.08	35.18±0.16
7	STANDH	26.85±0.15	26.57±0.14	26.48±0.02	26.85±0.03	25.93±0.15	24.46±0.08	23.63±0.22	25.93±0.17
8	WA	47.22±0.11	45.68±0.07	44.71±0.20	47.22±0.04	52.75±0.03	51.96±0.11	52.64±0.08	52.70±0.20

Table 4. Classification result of PD severity (%)

Act_Num	Activity_Name	KNN				XGB			
		Acc	F1	Pre	Rec	Acc	F1	Pre	Rec
1	FT	35.19±0.11	33.9±0.06	34.81±0.24	35.19±0.12	44.43±0.21	44.28±0.19	44.99±0.00	44.49±0.38
2	COA	53.75±0.15	52.32±0.17	55.44±0.30	53.71±0.23	55.53±0.08	54.86±0.07	54.77±0.17	55.52±0.15
3	ALTER	54.63±0.17	54.5±0.23	56.37±0.12	54.63±0.05	67.59±0.09	66.88±0.19	66.7±0.14	67.59±0.04
4	HR-R	44.44±0.07	43.31±0.15	44.73±0.23	44.45±0.20	54.63±0.09	53.67±0.31	54.29±0.09	54.63±0.23
5	HR-L	46.3±0.10	44.55±0.15	44.31±0.12	46.3±0.09	62.04±0.21	61.23±0.10	61.41±0.25	62.04±0.22
6	FN-R	38.89±0.16	36.65±0.10	37.94±0.14	38.89±0.21	57.41±0.15	57.83±0.29	58.93±0.26	57.41±0.23
7	STANDH	30.56±0.12	29.93±0.28	29.72±0.13	30.55±0.29	32.41±0.14	32.16±0.13	33±0.23	32.41±0.24
8	WA	53.7±0.19	52.39±0.13	52.6±0.08	53.7±0.15	48.15±0.13	47.25±0.08	47.52±0.19	48.15±0.17

3.4 Feature Dimensions

After sorting key features through the JMFS mechanism, we further explored the optimal feature dimension and identified the most useful features for disease diagnosis. Table 5 shows Comparison of accuracy in selecting features from different dimensions. We determine the optimal feature dimension by comparing the performance among different feature dimensions such as 10, 20, 30, and so on. This enables us to select the feature dimension that exhibits the best performance. The experimental results show that when retaining the most prominent features in the first 20 dimensions, the classification accuracy reaches the best 81.37%. Figure 4 shows the classification accuracy of different dimensional features on three activities, in these numerous experiments, it is found that all activities had the same trend, so only a portion of the activities were shown here. And it is more evident from the figure that the best classification performance is achieved when retaining the significance features of the top 20 dimensions.

Table 5. Comparison of accuracy for different feature dimensions (%)

Act_Num	Activity_Name	Dimensions		
		10	20	30
1	Finger taps	47.34	50.85	46.23
2	Clench and open alternately	63.12	67.12	62.36
3	Rapid alternating movements of hands	77.81	**81.37**	73.00
4	Hand rotation-right	65.90	69.04	65.72
5	Hand rotation-left	63.00	67.26	61.98
6	Finger to nose-right	54.12	56.58	54.65
7	Standing with arms hold	34.42	35.45	33.44
8	Walk back and forth	52.19	54.92	49.32

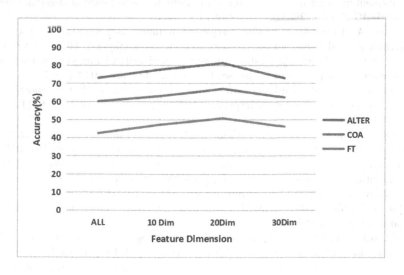

Fig. 4. Accuracy of different feature dimensions on three activities.

4   Conclusion

Accurately capturing motor symptom diagnosis of PD patients is particularly important to determining appropriate medication schedules. In this paper, we differentiate the PD severity and select representative 20 features related to the disease in 8 activities, which effectively provides more representative information than using all features. At present, the best accuracy is 20 dimensions features in ALTER, with an accuracy rate of 81.37%. This facilitate the later transplantation of lightweight equipment and provide reference for the independent PD diagnosis in the clinical or at home environment. In the future, we can test the possibility of more feature selection methods and an adaptive window sliding method which can be automatically adjusted according to the cycle of different activities themselves.

Acknowledgements. This research was supported by the National Natural Science Foundation of China (No. 62061050) and the 13th Postgraduate Research Innovation Project of Yunnan University 2021Y397. We thank Yunnan First People's Hospital for its strong support.

References

1. Abdel-Salam, R., Mostafa, R., Hadhood, M.: Human activity recognition using wearable sensors: review, challenges, evaluation benchmark. In: Li, X., Wu, M., Chen, Z., Zhang, L. (eds.) DL-HAR 2020. CCIS, vol. 1370, pp. 1–15. Springer, Singapore (2021). https://doi.org/10.1007/978-981-16-0575-8_1
2. AlMahadin, G., Lotfi, A., Zysk, E., Siena, F.L., Carthy, M.M., Breedon, P.: Parkinson's disease: current assessment methods and wearable devices for evaluation of movement disorder motor symptoms-a patient and healthcare professional perspective. BMC Neurol. **20**(1), 1–13 (2020)
3. Beuter, A., Edwards, R.: Using frequency domain characteristics to discriminate physiologic and parkinsonian tremors. J. Clin. Neurophysiol. **16**(5), 484 (1999)
4. Bovolenta, T.M., et al.: Systematic review and critical analysis of cost studies associated with parkinson's disease. Parkinson's Disease **2017** (2017)
5. Chén, O.Y., et al.: Building a machine-learning framework to remotely assess parkinson's disease using smartphones. IEEE Trans. Biomed. Eng. **67**(12), 3491–3500 (2020)
6. Deng, Z., Yang, P., Zhao, Y., Zhao, X., Dong, F.: Life-logging data aggregation solution for interdisciplinary healthcare research and collaboration. In: 2015 IEEE International Conference on Computer and Information Technology; Ubiquitous Computing and Communications; Dependable, Autonomic and Secure Computing; Pervasive Intelligence and Computing, pp. 2315–2320. IEEE (2015)
7. Dorsey, E., Sherer, T., Okun, M., Bloem, B.: The emerging evidence of the Parkinson pandemic. J. Parkinsons Dis. **8**(s1), S3–S8 (2018)
8. Erb, M.K., et al.: mhealth and wearable technology should replace motor diaries to track motor fluctuations in Parkinson's disease. NPJ Digit. Med. **3**(1), 6 (2020)
9. Fahn, S.: Description of parkinson's disease as a clinical syndrome. Ann. N. Y. Acad. Sci. **991**(1), 1–14 (2003)

10. Giuberti, M., Ferrari, G., Contin, L., Cimolin, V., Azzaro, C., Albani, G., Mauro, A.: Automatic updrs evaluation in the sit-to-stand task of parkinsonians: Kinematic analysis and comparative outlook on the leg agility task. IEEE J. Biomed. Health Inform. **19**(3), 803–814 (2015)
11. Goetz, C.G., et al.: Movement disorder society-sponsored revision of the unified Parkinson's disease rating scale (MDS-UPDRS): scale presentation and clinimetric testing results. Movem. Disord. Off. J. Movem. Disord. Soc. **23**(15), 2129–2170 (2008)
12. Guo, Y., Wang, L., Li, Y., Guo, L., Meng, F.: The detection of freezing of gait in Parkinson's disease using asymmetric basis function TV-ARMA time-frequency spectral estimation method. IEEE Trans. Neural Syst. Rehabil. Eng. **27**(10), 2077–2086 (2019)
13. Heijmans, M., Habets, J., Kuijf, M., Kubben, P., Herff, C.: Evaluation of Parkinson's disease at home: predicting tremor from wearable sensors. In: 2019 41st Annual International Conference of the IEEE Engineering in Medicine and Biology Society (EMBC), pp. 584–587. IEEE (2019)
14. Hubble, R.P., Naughton, G.A., Silburn, P.A., Cole, M.H.: Wearable sensor use for assessing standing balance and walking stability in people with Parkinson's disease: a systematic review. PLoS ONE **10**(4), e0123705 (2015)
15. Kim, J.W., et al.: Quantification of bradykinesia during clinical finger taps using a Gyrosensor in patients with Parkinson's disease. Med. Biol. Eng. Comput. **49**, 365–371 (2011)
16. Lara, O.D., Labrador, M.A.: A survey on human activity recognition using wearable sensors. IEEE Commun. Surv. Tutor. **15**(3), 1192–1209 (2012)
17. Liu, K., Wang, R.: Antisaturation adaptive fixed-time sliding mode controller design to achieve faster convergence rate and its application. IEEE Trans. Circuits Syst. II Express Briefs **69**(8), 3555–3559 (2022)
18. Liu, K., Yang, P., Wang, R., Jiao, L., Li, T., Zhang, J.: Observer-based adaptive fuzzy finite-time attitude control for quadrotor UAVs. IEEE Trans. Aerosp. Electron. Syst. (2023)
19. Long, D., et al.: Automatic classification of early Parkinson's disease with multimodal MR imaging. PLoS ONE **7**(11), e47714 (2012)
20. Maetzler, W., Domingos, J., Srulijes, K., Ferreira, J.J., Bloem, B.R.: Quantitative wearable sensors for objective assessment of parkinson's disease. Mov. Disord. **28**(12), 1628–1637 (2013)
21. Patel, S., et al.: Monitoring motor fluctuations in patients with Parkinson's disease using wearable sensors. IEEE Trans. Inf. Technol. Biomed. **13**(6), 864–873 (2009)
22. Perez-Ibarra, J.C., Siqueira, A.A., Krebs, H.I.: Identification of gait events in healthy subjects and with Parkinson's disease using inertial sensors: an adaptive unsupervised learning approach. IEEE Trans. Neural Syst. Rehabil. Eng. **28**(12), 2933–2943 (2020)
23. Rayan, Z., Alfonse, M., Salem, A.B.M.: Machine learning approaches in smart health. Procedia Comput. Sci. **154**, 361–368 (2019)
24. Rovini, E., Maremmani, C., Cavallo, F.: How wearable sensors can support parkinson's disease diagnosis and treatment: a systematic review. Front. Neurosci. **11**, 555 (2017)
25. San-Segundo, R., Blunck, H., Moreno-Pimentel, J., Stisen, A., Gil-Martín, M.: Robust human activity recognition using smartwatches and smartphones. Eng. Appl. Artif. Intell. **72**, 190–202 (2018)
26. Schlachetzki, J.C., et al.: Wearable sensors objectively measure gait parameters in Parkinson's disease. PLoS ONE **12**(10), e0183989 (2017)

27. Shcherbak, A., Kovalenko, E., Somov, A.: Detection and classification of early stages of Parkinson's disease through wearable sensors and machine learning. IEEE Trans. Instrument. Measur. (2023)
28. Shulman, L.M., Gruber-Baldini, A.L., Anderson, K.E., Fishman, P.S., Reich, S.G., Weiner, W.J.: The clinically important difference on the unified Parkinson's disease rating scale. Arch. Neurol. **67**(1), 64–70 (2010)
29. Sigcha, L., et al.: Bradykinesia detection in Parkinson's disease using smartwatches' inertial sensors and deep learning methods. Electronics **11**(23), 3879 (2022)
30. Spanakis, E.G., et al.: Myhealthavatar: personalized and empowerment health services through internet of things technologies. In: 2014 4th International Conference on Wireless Mobile Communication and Healthcare-Transforming Healthcare Through Innovations in Mobile and Wireless Technologies (MOBIHEALTH), pp. 331–334. IEEE (2014)
31. Suzuki, M., Mitoma, H., Yoneyama, M., et al.: Quantitative analysis of motor status in Parkinson's disease using wearable devices: from methodological considerations to problems in clinical applications. Parkinson's Dis. **2017** (2017)
32. Ullrich, M., et al.: Detection of unsupervised standardized gait tests from real-world inertial sensor data in Parkinson's disease. IEEE Trans. Neural Syst. Rehabil. Eng. **29**, 2103–2111 (2021)
33. Wang, X., Qi, J., Yang, Y., Yang, P.: A survey of disease progression modeling techniques for Alzheimer's diseases. In: 2019 IEEE 17th International Conference on Industrial Informatics (INDIN), vol. 1, pp. 1237–1242. IEEE (2019)
34. Yang, P., Yang, C., Lanfranchi, V., Ciravegna, F.: Activity graph based convolutional neural network for human activity recognition using acceleration and gyroscope data. IEEE Trans. Industr. Inf. **18**(10), 6619–6630 (2022)
35. Yang, P., et al.: DUAPM: a effective dynamic micro-blogging user activity prediction model towards cyber-physical-social systems. IEEE Trans. Industr. Inf. **16**(8), 5317–5326 (2019)

Author Index

A
Alaba, Adebola 14

C
Chang, Xiangchao 69
Chen, Jianjun 111
Chen, Jing 84
Chen, Qi 29

D
De, Suparna 29

E
Eziefuna, Ebere 14

G
Garcia, David 1

H
Henrikson, Shane 1
Huang, Kaizhu 29

J
Jian, Yihui 84
Jiang, Wengyao 111
Jin, Ziguan 84

L
Li, Chenxi 41, 102
Li, Tao 41, 102
Li, Youyong 41
Li, Ziheng 124
Ling, Xinrui 84
Liu, Chang 94
Liu, Jingjing 94
Liu, Kang 41, 52
Liu, Tong 52
Liu, Zhangdaihong 94
Lv, Lulu 41, 102

M
Mao, Kaitai 84

N
Nan, Fengtao 124
Nguyen, Anh 29

P
Peng, Xiyang 52, 124

Q
Qi, Jun 52, 111
Qin, Yuxin 102

S
Sarafrazi, Soodabeh 1
Sharif, Naveed 1
Shen, Yixiao 111

W
Wang, Wei 29, 111
Wang, Xulong 52, 124
Wang, Yuqi 29
Wang, Zeqiang 29
Wheeler, Darwin 1
Wu, Hui 1

X
Xu, Jingzhou 111
Xu, Kaichen 84

Y
Yang, Geng 84
Yang, Jiawei 41, 102
Yang, Po 52, 69, 124
Yang, Yang 94
Yang, Yun 69, 124

J. Qi and P. Yang (Eds.): IoTBDH 2023, CCIS 2019, pp. 137–138, 2024.
https://doi.org/10.1007/978-3-031-52216-1

Ye, Zhiqiu 84
Yu, Hong Qing 14
Yu, Hongqing 41
Yuan, Zhipeng 41, 52
Yue, Peng 124

Z
Zhang, Qin 84
Zhang, Yu 52
Zhao, Yuting 124
Zhao, Zhong 124
Zhou, Menghui 52, 69, 124

Printed in the United States
by Baker & Taylor Publisher Services